Anonymous

The Lord's Offering

Or, the exchange of the kingdom, and the Church's exchequer. Being the essays on systematic beneficence to which have been awarded the prizes offered by the synod of the United Presbyterian Church in May 1875

Anonymous

The Lord's Offering
Or, the exchange of the kingdom, and the Church's exchequer. Being the essays on systematic beneficence to which have been awarded the prizes offered by the synod of the United Presbyterian Church in May 1875

ISBN/EAN: 9783337183639

Printed in Europe, USA, Canada, Australia, Japan

Cover: Foto ©Lupo / pixelio.de

More available books at **www.hansebooks.com**

The Lord's Offering:

OR

THE EXCHANGE OF THE KINGDOM,

AND

THE CHURCH'S EXCHEQUER;

BEING THE

ESSAYS ON SYSTEMATIC BENEFICENCE TO WHICH HAVE
BEEN AWARDED THE PRIZES OFFERED BY THE
SYNOD OF THE UNITED PRESBYTERIAN
CHURCH IN MAY 1875.

EDINBURGH: ANDREW ELLIOT.
LONDON: JAMES NISBET & CO.

MDCCCLXXVII.

PRIZE ESSAYS ON SYSTEMATIC BENEFICENCE.

DESIRING to foster in the Churches the spirit of Christian liberality and the practice of systematic beneficence, three Elders of the United Presbyterian Church recently placed at the disposal of the Synod of that Church the sum of £150, in order that two Prizes might be offered for Essays on the principles of systematic, proportionate, and frequent giving to the cause of Christ. The Synod remitted the consideration of this proposal to the Home Committee of its Board of Missions, and that Committee have arranged that a Prize of £100 shall be offered for the best, and a second Prize of £50 for the second best Essay on the subject. The Essays are not to exceed in length 120 printed pages 8vo; and it is expected that they shall contain a full and persuasive statement of the Scriptural argument in favour of systematic, proportionate, and frequent contribution for religious and benevolent purposes, and of the advantages which would accrue to the givers themselves, and to the Church, from the practical application of that argument to the determination of the proportion of means and income which ought to be devoted by each individual to the Lord.

In accordance with the wishes of the Donors of the Prize Fund, the Competition is open to all Ministers on the Synod Rolls of the United Presbyterian Church, and of the Presbyterian Church in England:—and the Rev. Professor LORIMER, of the English Presbyterian College, London; the Rev. Dr JOHN KER, of Sydney Place Church, Glasgow; and the Rev. ANDREW THOMSON, of Broughton Place Church, Edinburgh, have engaged to act as adjudicators of the Prizes.

The manuscripts are to be sent to the Rev. ROBERT SELKIRK SCOTT, D.D., at the Offices of the United Presbyterian Church, 66 Virginia Street, Glasgow, on or before the 1st May 1876; and it is expected that the award may be given on the 1st August 1876. Each Essay is to have a Motto written upon it, and to be accompanied by a sealed Envelope, bearing the same Motto, and containing the Name and Address of the Author.

As the successful Essays may afterwards be published for cheap or gratuitous circulation, they are to belong to the Home Committee of the United Presbyterian Board of Missions, and to be disposed of by that Committee as they may deem best.

On behalf of the Donors and the Committee,

ROBERT S. SCOTT, *Secretary.*

GLASGOW, 24*th November* 1875.

AWARD OF THE ADJUDICATORS.

LONDON, 21st October 1876.

Having undertaken to act as Adjudicators of the two Prizes offered by the Home Committee of the Board of Missions of the United Presbyterian Church for Essays "On the Principles of Systematic, Proportionate, and Frequent Giving for the Cause of Christ," we have read and examined with due care the Essays which have been submitted to our inspection, and we have been able to arrive without difficulty at a unanimous judgment in favour of the two Essays bearing respectively the following mottoes :—

    (1) Δωρεὰν ἐλάβετε, δωρεὰν δότε.
    (2) We can all do more than we have done,
        And not be a whit the worse :
        It never was loving that emptied the heart,
        Or giving that emptied the purse.

To (1) we are agreed in adjudicating the prize of £100 ; and
To (2) the prize of £50.

We have found these two Essays of nearly equal merit, though in different respects ; but there is a sufficient degree of superiority in No. 1 to turn the scale.

The writer of the first is the Rev. ALEXANDER M. DALRYMPLE, M.A., Smethwick, Birmingham. The writer of the second is the Rev. ALEXANDER M. SYMINGTON, B.A., Birkenhead. Other two Essays, nearest in merit to the two best, were found worthy of honourable mention.

The Prize Essays will be found to contain what it was desired and expected they should—viz., "A full and persuasive statement of the scriptural argument in favour of systematic, proportionate, and frequent contribution for religious and benevolent purposes, and of the advantages which would accrue to the givers themselves and to the Church from the practical application of that argument to the determination of the proportion of means and income which ought to be devoted by each individual to the Lord."

Much of the exposition and the reasoning employed by the Authors will be fresh and striking to many ; and we do not doubt that both papers will leave a strong impression of the value and importance of the principles of Christian giving for which they plead. Their publication will be specially seasonable at the present time, when there is so hopeful a movement in progress among the Churches in the direction of *united* work in the service of the common Master ; for such united work can best be done when the workers are "perfectly joined together in one mind and one judgment" touching the Lord's own revealed will as to the best modes of doing it.

                PETER LORIMER, D.D.
                ANDREW THOMSON, D.D.
                JOHN KER, D.D.

PREFACE.

The Advertisement and the Award of the Adjudicators, which are printed on the preceding pages, indicate the origin and the design of the two Essays which are now submitted to the attention and consideration of the Christian public, and leave little to be added by way of preface.

In May 1875, three elders in connection with the United Presbyterian Church, who were then in attendance at the meeting of the Synod of that Church at Edinburgh, submitted to the Home Mission Secretary a proposal for placing at the disposal of the Synod the sum of One hundred and fifty pounds, in order that two Prizes might be offered for Essays to be written by ministers on Systematic Beneficence. It was the desire of these gentlemen in making this proposal to foster the spirit of Christian liberality among the members of Christian Churches; and so to present to their consideration the scriptural authority, and the manifold advantages of systematic, frequent, and proportionate giving to the cause of Christ, as to furnish motives and inducements for adopting and carrying into effect the principle of giving habitually and conscientiously in proportion to means and income, instead of contributing fitfully and uncertainly under the influence of present impulse or personal solicitation.

When this proposal was brought under the notice of the Synod, it was cordially approved and accepted, and the Home Committee of the Synod's Board of Missions were directed to make the necessary arrangements for the public offer of the prizes. It was accordingly agreed that a prize of £100 should be offered for the best, and a second prize of £50 for the second best, essay on the subject; and, in accordance with the wishes of the donors of the prize fund, the competition was declared open to all ministers whose names were placed on the Synod rolls of the United Presbyterian Church, and of the Presbyterian Church in (now, of) England. It was specially required that the Essays should contain a clear and comprehensive statement of the Scriptural argument in favour of system and proportion in the application of property or income to religious and benevolent purposes; and that they should exhibit in an attractive and persuasive form the advantages which may be expected to accrue to the givers themselves, and to the cause of Jesus Christ in the world, from the practical application of that argument to the regulation of individual conduct and contribution, and for the determination of the proportion of his income which each should consecrate to the Lord.

The Rev. Professor Lorimer of London, the Rev. John Ker, D.D., of Glasgow, and the Rev. Andrew Thomson, D.D., of Edinburgh, were requested to act as adjudicators of the prizes, and cheerfully undertook that duty. The

Essays were accordingly forwarded to them, and after careful consideration of the claims and merits of the several papers, they at length unanimously agreed to award the First Prize of £100 to the Essay which bore the motto " Δωρεὰν ἐλάβετε, δωρεὰν δότε;" and the Second Prize of £50 to the Essay which bore the motto,

> " We can all do more than we have done,
> And not be a whit the worse ;
> It never was loving that emptied the heart,
> Or giving that emptied the purse."

On opening the sealed letters which accompanied these Essays, it was found that the first had been written by the Rev. Alexander M. Dalrymple, M.A., minister of the United Presbyterian Congregation at Smethwick, near Birmingham, and that he therefore had obtained the First Prize ; and that the second had been written by the Rev. Alexander M. Symington, B.A., minister of the Presbyterian Church in England, at Birkenhead, to whom consequently the Second Prize was awarded.

The adjudicators all concur in testifying to the general excellence of the Essays submitted to them for examination, and in stating that the two Essays next in order to those to which the prizes were awarded were entitled to be mentioned with honour. They also concur in the expression of the hope and the assurance that the perusal of the two Prize Essays will be found interesting and profitable throughout the Churches, and that their statements and appeals will present the duty of frequent and proportional giving for benevolent and religious purposes in such new and powerful lights as must lead to a more intelligent and conscientious consecration of income and of substance for the promotion of human welfare and of the divine glory; and thus to the attainment of the end which the generous donors of the prize fund had in view in the proposal which they submitted to the Synod of the Church in 1875.

Through the considerate kindness of the donors of the prizes, a copy of the volume containing both the Essays will be presented to the Minister and to the Session Clerk of each of the congregations included in the Synod Rolls of the United Presbyterian Church, and of the Presbyterian Church of England; and as the aim of the donors and of the Synod is to diffuse information as widely as possible on the important subject to which the Essays refer, the volume, and also the separate essays, will be published at the lowest possible price which will cover the cost of production. It is hoped, therefore, that ministers, office-bearers, and members of Christian Churches may lend their willing and effective aid in bringing these Essays under the notice of the Christian community; and they are now sent forth from the press with the desire and prayer that, through the divine blessing, they may be made instrumental in advancing the truth and cause of Him who is "worthy to receive riches," and to whom "shall be given of the gold of Sheba."

R. S. S.

THE EXCHANGE OF THE KINGDOM.

A

CONTENTS.

CHAP.		PAGE.
I.—THE CHURCH'S MISSION	. . . .	5
II.—THE CHURCH'S AGENCIES	. . .	15
III.—THE SCRIPTURE ACCOUNT OF THE DUTY OF GIVING TO GOD	. . . . . .	32
IV.—SCRIPTURE ILLUSTRATIONS OF THE DUTY	. .	48
V.—THE CHURCH'S OBLIGATION TO GIVE	. .	60
VI.—EXISTING METHODS AND THEIR RESULTS	. .	78
VII.—A MORE EXCELLENT WAY	. . . .	100
VIII.—PROSPERITY	. . . . .	126
IX.—HIGHER CHRISTIAN LIFE	. . . .	142

THE EXCHANGE OF THE KINGDOM.

CHAPTER I.

THE CHURCH'S MISSION.

THE Christian religion urges to strenuous effort all who sincerely profess it. Other forms of belief have been found compatible with a comfortable acquiescence in the existing state of things, but the genuine Christian has always partaken of the character ascribed to the founders of his faith, of whom it was said that they were men who had turned the world upside down. Dissatisfaction deep and constant has a certain place in the heart of every Christian. His own spiritual condition does not suggest to him any complacent thoughts. He is too sensible that he has not yet attained to the standard of the perfect man in Christ Jesus, and he is impelled, "forgetting those things which are behind," to "reach forth unto those things which are before." His zeal for the purity and the progress of the church excites in him a generous impatience of all that tends to mar the one, or to interfere with the other. Love to his fellowmen kindles indignation and pity by turns in his breast. And by all these emotions he is perpetually urged to efforts after amelioration or reform.

In the New Testament we have two remarkable statements of the purpose of Christ's mission which fully account for the irrepressible and unappeasable character of the religion which He founded. "For this purpose the Son of God was manifested, that He might destroy the works of the devil." "I am come that ye might have life, and that ye might have it more abundantly." The annihilation of all evil, the building up of all good,—nothing less than this will satisfy the demands of Christianity. Sin, which is the cause of spiritual, moral and physical disease, must be eradicated, and every principle capable of bearing fruit unto life must be carefully tended and nurtured, until the prophetic vision is realised, and "instead of the thorn shall come up the fir tree, and instead of the brier shall come up the myrtle tree;"—until "the wilderness and the solitary place shall be glad for them; and the desert shall rejoice, and blossom as the rose."

Our Lord had habitually before Him, both in His hours of contemplation and in His hours of action, two worlds; the actual world of sin, sorrow and suffering, and His own ideal world of the redeemed. At the outset of His ministry He was tempted to acquiescence in the actual, by the most magnificent promise ever held out to man on earth, "All these things (all the kingdoms of the world and the glory of them) will I give Thee, if thou wilt fall down and worship me." But He repudiated the idea of acquiescence with holy indignation. And when during His ministry the actual state of the world was brought before Him in thought, it never failed to touch deep wells of feeling. "When He saw the multitudes, He was moved with compassion." "When He was come near, He beheld the city, and wept over it." Even in the dark hour of His own passion we find Him saying, "Daughters of Jerusalem, weep not for Me; but weep for yourselves, and for your children." The hypocrisy, the oppression, the selfishness prevalent in the world inspired Him now with indignation, now with pity, and drew from Him alternately words of withering rebuke and of tender expostulation.

On the other hand, in His hours of solitude and prayer, there arose before Him a vision of marvellous beauty,—the Kingdom of God. Its coming would be noiseless and without pomp. "The Kingdom of God cometh not with observation." It would come first in the souls of men. "The Kingdom of God is within you." But its influence would radiate from its possessors on all sides. "Ye are the light of the world." "Ye are the salt of the earth." That influence would deepen and extend until it would leaven the world. Wherever the Kingdom was established men would be blessed. Holiness and happiness would together take possession of the soul of the individual, and permeate society. To secure such results no labour, no expense could be too great. He himself would freely give His life, a ransom for many. The Kingdom of God was the pearl of great price, to acquire which a man might reasonably part with all his possessions. No satisfaction found in the enjoyment of this world's goods could be equal to the inward peace and joy of a soul which had entered the Kingdom. Sacrifice for the Kingdom's sake was true wisdom. One might shrink from losing a right eye or a right hand, but the prospect of entrance into life might well reconcile men to even greater sacrifices than these. Rank and power, wealth and luxury, reputation for religiousness would have no power to dazzle eyes rejoicing in the clear light of the glory that excelleth. Such being the views of Christ respecting the Kingdom of God, we are not surprised that the burden of all His teaching should be, *Strive to enter in.*

Turning our attention to the activities of the Saviour's life we find them all directed to the two-fold end already indicated, the overthrow of evil, the establishment and diffusion of good. "He went about doing good." "He healed every sickness and every disease among the people." "He spake as none other man spake." "The common people heard Him gladly." Of His life-work He himself gave this compendious account, "The blind receive their sight, and the lame walk, the lepers are cleansed, and the deaf hear, the dead are raised up, and the poor have the gospel preached to them."

While engaged in these labours of love and continuing in them up to the point of exhaustion, an oppressive sense of the greatness of the work to be done and of the indifference of the world to it, overpowered Him, and we find Him thus appealing to His disciples, "The harvest truly is plenteous, but the labourers are few. Pray ye therefore the Lord of the harvest, that He will send forth labourers into His harvest." The training, equipment and commissioning of such labourers occupied much of Christ's thoughts and of His care. From time to time while He continued with His disciples, He sent them out on journeys of preaching and healing. And when, having accomplished His great sacrificial work, He was about to leave them, to take His seat on the throne of heaven, He invested them with the ample and urgent commission, "Go ye into all the world, and preach the gospel to every creature."

The Church which inherits the unsearchable riches of Christ is also the executor of His will, and upon it devolves the prosecution of the two-fold work of overthrow and of reconstruction which He began. No words could be plainer, as none could be more solemn, than those in which Christ bequeathed this legacy of duty to His disciples. While He was with them He frequently impressed upon them their responsibilities. In the parable of the talents He taught them to regard themselves as His servants, and to consider their duty, their happiness, and their highest interests as all consisting in the energetic carrying on of the work which lay so near His heart. And when about to leave them His profound interest in that work and deep anxiety respecting it were manifested by the frequency of His appeals to them on its behalf, and by the greatness of the encouragements He held out to them. Among other stimulating declarations, He assured them that He would Himself be with them, and that unprecedented success would attend their efforts. "The works that I do shall ye do also; and greater works than these shall ye do; because I go unto my Father."

The Church when realising its Founder's idea is thus essentially a society for practical work in the world. It is committed to a policy of universal, constant, and endless exertion. It is true that this effort springs from, and is directed by, a sublime faith which lays hold of heaven and hell. It is true that Christianity has its speculative as well as its practical aims. The Church has its creed and its theology and these are intimately and inseparably associated with its active service. But the grand ends which it is bound to propose to itself are the ends pursued by its Founder, the destruction of the works of the devil, and the giving of life and yet more abundant life to men. To these ends the divine truth embodied in its creeds and theological systems is itself subservient. The achievement of these ends, and not a profession of faith, which may or may not be sincere and real, is made by Christ the proof of discipleship. "By their fruits ye shall know them." In proportion as a man leaves the world better than he found it, by the amendment of his own life, by having waged war against ignorance, selfishness, tyranny and disorder, and by having defended and advocated the principles of truth and love, in such measure has he obeyed the command, "Follow me." Isolation from the world, even when sought with a view to the consecration of time and strength to worship and meditation, cannot plead either the example or the sanction of Christ. And when indifference to the wellbeing of society springs from selfish absorption in personal aims, it is utterly repugnant to His spirit, and in disregard of His most earnest desires. Watching and prayer are indeed enjoined by Him, and temporary retirement from the world to secure time and leisure for these is needful; but the end of such exercises is the renewal of strength, and the clearing of spiritual vision, for more strenuous conflicts with evil and more abundant labours to promote the Good.

The great gospel commission bore upon it an instruction to the disciples to begin at Jerusalem. So, when Christ calls men to labour for Him now, the field into which He first sends them is that of their own hearts, and to it attention must be directed to the last. Those who would enlist in Christ's service for the reformation of the world must begin by reforming themselves. "To work out one's own salvation with fear and trembling," to seek personally "to be no longer conformed to this world, but to be transformed by the renewing of the mind, and to prove what is that good and acceptable and perfect will of God," this is not only the first contribution required of those who would help on the Kingdom, but one without the preliminary rendering of which no other is of any value. "A corrupt tree cannot bring forth good fruit." If the heart of a man be not right with God his acts of proffered service and his gifts have no acceptability. Even the ploughing of the wicked is sin. A want of integrity in character, or of purity in motive, generally imparts some element of weakness even to deeds professedly religious or philanthropic. Such faultiness often reveals itself in a surprising manner even after a long interval; and it is not difficult thus to explain, on natural grounds, how it so frequently happens that the little given or done by a righteous man is more greatly blessed than the imposing offerings of many wicked. It is not to be denied that God sometimes accomplishes good by means of those who have themselves neither part nor lot in His inheritance. The Apostle Paul clearly leads us to infer that one may even preach the gospel to others and yet be himself a castaway. But it still remains true that the measure of usefulness in advancing the Kingdom in the world is determined chiefly by the extent to which it already exists in the heart of the worker. "My son give me thine heart," is Christ's first demand, and only after the heart has been surrendered to Him does He call us to engage in His service. Too much stress cannot be laid on the divinely appointed order by which personal consecration is made to precede service, and to be the condition of its acceptability and in general the measure of its success. Many ostentatious and loudly-trumpeted schemes have come to naught, or have failed to bear fruit commensurate with their promise, because this order has been neglected. Care has been lavished only on organization and machinery. The motive fires of Christian love and hope have been suffered to burn low, or to expire. Much will be said hereafter respecting the duty of giving liberally for the supply of the Lord's treasury, and it is the more necessary strongly to insist here on the truth that "to obey is better than sacrifice, and to hearken than the fat of rams." The feeblest cry of a penitent soul for mercy, the humblest act of loyal submission to the divine will, are in the eyes of God incalculably more precious than untold treasures heaped upon His altar but unsanctified by the spirit of devotion.

When men have responded to Christ's gracious invitation, "Come," then it is He sends them forth to carry that invitation to others. "Go," He said, when on earth, to one whom He had blessed, "tell thy friends how great things the Lord hath done for thee, and hath had compassion on thee." And the heart of the converted sinner eagerly answers to this intimation of the Saviour's will. Gratitude, the joy of deliverance, and the thrillings of a new life, all impel him to seek the extension to others of the blessings he has himself received. In the ardour of a first love he scarcely waits to hear the proclamation, "Whom shall I send, and who will go for us?" but hastens to present himself with the petition, "Here am I, send me." Would that this ardour were constant and universal! Assuredly Christ has a right to expect it.

It is no part of our design to present an extended view of the present condition of the world, in order to indicate the work which still remains to be done for Christ. But the most hasty survey of that work suffices to reveal its gigantic proportions. It is probable that nine hundred millions of the twelve hundred millions of the race have not even heard the name of Him who is mighty to save. They are still walking in darkness and dwelling in the land of the shadow of death. And of those three hundred millions who inhabit so-called Christian countries, there are millions who disown the designation 'Christian,' and many millions more to whom the most liberally charitable would hesitate to accord it. Within the borders of our own land, pre-eminent as its privileges and opportunities have been, how far is the religion of Jesus Christ from being universally accepted and obeyed. The kingdom of the Evil One, alas! still stands, flaunting its defiance of all who would attempt its overthrow; and the ignorance, the superstition, the infidelity, the intemperance, and the licentiousness which prevail bear melancholy but indubitable testimony to its stability and its power. Sometimes when contemplating the vastness of the field to be subdued, and considering how much more rapid and luxuriant the growth of error is than that of truth, we are tempted to despond, and are ready to ask, if eighteen centuries of prayer and work have resulted only in what we now see, how long must the Kingdom tarry, or rather what hope is there of its appearance? But God is faithful who has promised, and the Church continuing patiently and believingly to sow in tears shall yet reap in joy. Meantime it is all-important to bear in mind that not one earnest word or deed is without its influence in hastening on the glorious consummation, small as progress in the aggregate may seem to be. It becomes every Christian therefore to be about his Lord's business, diligently, zealously, hopefully; "occupying" till he come.

One reservation has already been made, to the effect that the homage of the heart is more highly esteemed by God than the most laborious services and the costliest offerings unsanctified by right motives; and, before entering on the special subject of this essay, another must be added, namely, that personal work for Christ is service of a higher order than the giving of money in order that work may be done by others. To give is a duty, an important duty, and one respecting which we have much to say, but in urging liberality we must not lose sight of this, that no faithfulness in giving can justly be urged as an excuse for neglecting the other and still higher service of seeking by one's own words and deeds to advance the cause of Christ and the welfare of man. All are not called to be pastors or teachers, evangelists or missionaries, but on every one the injunction is laid to adorn the doctrine of God his Saviour, and to show out of a good conversation, his works with meekness of wisdom.

We have thus stated our view of the nature of the Church's mission, and of the part to be taken in fulfilling it by every Christian. That mission is in short to overthrow all powers of darkness and to establish the Kingdom of God. The individual believer rightly begins by rendering a personal submission, and then proceeds to active personal service, completing his round of duty and privilege by giving of his substance as God has prospered him for the carrying on of these great works.

It is this last branch of Christian obligation which we propose to consider here somewhat fully. If we would profitably study it, and be guided to wise and just conclusions, we must approach it in the spirit of faith and love, and above all we must seek to bear clearly in mind the high nature of the issue at stake, which is nothing less than the successful prosecution of those great ends for which our beloved Redeemer and Master lived and died, and the continued care of which He has solemnly entrusted to His Church. The salvation of immortal souls, the physical and moral well-being of the human family, the restoration of peace to the earth, the fulfilment of the joy of the Lord and the completion of His crown, these and no less are the results, which in the providence of God, have been permitted to depend so largely on the faithfulness of the Church. Let every

Christian pray that the clear, earnest, loving, self-sacrificing mind which was in Christ may be in him also. Let him seek like his Master to contemplate the woe of lost souls and to compassionate them. Let him seek to have before him, on the one hand, the awful sum of human guilt and misery, and on the other, the beatific vision of the Kingdom of God yet to be established in power and glory on the earth. And let him consider that to him a post in the great conflict has been assigned, that he wields power, and that he is responsible for its use. And then when the daily prayer is sent up, "Thy Kingdom come," let him ask whether by self-consecration, or personal service, or cheerfully offered and liberal gifts, he has come to the help of the Lord against the mighty, and contributed to the speedier advent of that joyful day, when it shall be proclaimed, "The kingdoms of this world are become the kingdoms of our Lord and of His Christ: and He shall reign for ever and ever."

CHAPTER II.

THE CHURCH'S AGENCIES.

THE great and beneficent ends which the Church, in accordance with its Founder's example and precept, proposes to itself, are to be attained by the use of means which are often humble and apparently inadequate. There is an analogy, in this respect, between God's work of creation and His work of providence. And when doubt arises in our minds as to whether spiritual ends arrived at through the intervention of means so ordinary and human can be of divine appointment, it may be removed by a thoughtful consideration of this analogy. In nature, the gigantic is frequently developed from the minute, the useful is found to be absolutely dependent upon what might at first sight appear to be the useless, and forms full of beauty and strength spring from matter which has no pretension to either. We ought not, therefore, to be surprised or disturbed in mind on finding that such lofty spiritual results as the salvation of lost souls and the restoration of the human family to original holiness and happiness are, at a certain link in the chain of cause and effect, made to depend on the labours and self-denial of men themselves, and that even material forces, such as the silver and the gold of commerce, are factors in the final result. Scripture assures us repeatedly that it is the delight and glory of God to employ, for the carrying out of his mighty purposes, means which by men are rejected and despised. "It pleased God, by the foolishness of preaching, to save them that believe." "God hath chosen the foolish things of the world to confound the wise; and God hath chosen the weak things of the world to confound the things which are mighty; and base things of the world, and things which are despised, hath God chosen, and things which are not, to bring to nought things that are." "We have this treasure in earthen vessels, that the excellency of the power may be of God, and not of us."

It cannot be questioned that many are prone to disparage the means which God delights to use, and thus to honour. And unhappily this class of objectors does not consist exclusively of persons outside of the Church. Some who would be indignant if their Christianity were called in question are yet constantly setting up their own standards of right, and their own ideas of fitness, in opposition to the plain and oft-repeated intimations of

God's will in the Scriptures. There is an inflated, fantastic, and at heart selfish, pietism, which professes to find pleasure in the contemplation of spiritual ends, but which at once collapses when questions are raised respecting the means of their accomplishment. Those whose Christianity is of this texture generally belong to the class of " hearers of the word and not doers." They are skilled in detecting the weak points of church organization, and they can inveigh most eloquently against those responsible and hardworking organizers, by the 'materialism' of whose notions and schemes they are offended. Congregational arrangements, missionary enterprises, Sunday schools, town missions, charitable societies and institutions, all find in them minute and painstaking critics. Far from cultivating the spirit of Him of whom it was predicted that He would not 'break the bruised reed nor quench the smoking flax,' they despise the day of small things, and fall with great swelling words of spiritual sound upon the simple and sincere worker in the cause, discouraging him with representations of the futility of his efforts and the inefficiency of his plans. They are too proud or too indolent to work in the vineyard themselves, and to do whatever work the Master may appoint. If an opportunity were afforded them of doing some great thing which would bring name and fame, they would probably be ready enough, but as it is, they stand idly at the gate, not entering themselves, and hindering those who would enter. With especial harshness does the word 'money' grate upon the ears of such cavillers, when it is referred to as being required in the service of God. Forgetting, apparently, to how large an extent the Scriptures treat of money, both as employed for personal uses and as devoted to the purposes of religion, they are ready, if not to hold up their hands and to exclaim, Profanation! at least to mutter and whisper to a similar effect. And it is extremely probable that the charge in their mouths has the merit of consistency, if not of fairness; the only idea which many such persons have of money being that it is a purveyor to selfish gratification, and accordingly to be eagerly pursued, carefully retained, and selfishly expended, not one noble or generous sentiment attending it from first to last, either in acquisition or in outlay. If this were truly the essential and unalterable character of money, it would indeed be 'vile trash,' and such as never could be an acceptable offering on God's altar. But money does not always thus bear the impress of a selfish and ignoble nature. It may have stamped upon it the character of a true, ardent, self-sacrificing human heart; and in such a case even money is accepted of the Lord, and the loving heart of the giver sanctifies the gift. But to all such objectors it is sufficient to reply that God himself has sanctioned, and indeed appointed, the use of earthly instrumentalities for the attainment of spiritual ends; so it has seemed good in His sight. The foolishness of God is here as elsewhere wiser than men, and when Christ's people, setting aside all vain and self-originated notions, apply themselves with common sense and diligence to the doing of every good work that the hand finds to do, including the humblest offices of help to their fellowmen among those to which they are called by the Master, they will find that in all such labour there is profit, and Wisdom will be justified of her children.

We must now proceed to a very rapid survey of the principal agencies employed by the Church in promoting the Kingdom of Christ, that we may have clearer ideas as to what may be required to maintain them in efficiency. By God all powers are overruled for the advancement of his great purposes. Civilization, commerce, political revolutions, and even war, have been instruments in his hands for breaking down barriers which have obstructed the Gospel, and for paving a way along which it might pass to peoples the most remote. He makes even the wrath of man to redound to His praise, and the cupidity of the merchant, the turbulence of the demagogue, the ambition of the soldier, not less than the laudable inquisitiveness of the natural philosopher, have been made subservient to beneficent purposes, than which none were more remote from the minds of the unwitting agents. But at present we have to do only with the efforts put forth by the Church itself for the express purpose of furthering the interests of religion; and without professing to give an exhaustive account of the agencies which it employs, we may specify as the most important, the Pulpit, the Press, Education, Almsgiving, and the support of Benevolent Institutions.

Among these, the first place must be assigned to the provision made for the conduct of an intelligent and spiritual worship; and in this we include both the erection of churches and the education and due maintenance of an able ministry. It is no part of our plan to enter into an elaborate defence of the gospel ministry as it exists in the Church in modern times. We hold that the institution is in accordance with the dictates of sound sense, and that it is supported by the authority of Scripture. Objections to the setting apart of a ministerial order have never received much favour; and those who have given their scruples practical effect, by abolishing the sacred office, have often been driven by necessity to restore it under some other form or name. The Church being the light of the world, its first duties are to guard the purity and to maintain the brightness of its own spiritual illumination, to hand down the truth inviolate and unimpaired from generation to generation, and to secure the universal diffusion of that truth among its members, so that the word of God dwelling in them richly, they may be thoroughly furnished to all good works. These are offices which demand unremitting attention and ceaseless labour. The work is also of paramount importance as bearing on evangelization, for when the Church is rich in faith, in virtue, and in knowledge, the candle burns brightly in the candlestick, and its benignant rays draw the attention of a world lying in darkness. The Scriptures abound in passages descriptive of the blessings which flow to a church from its possession of true and faithful prophets or teachers, and the curse involved in being deprived of them. "Where no vision is the people perish." In the warnings addressed to false, self-seeking and time-serving prophets, and the terrible denunciations of their unfaithfulness, as well as in the blessings pronounced upon the faithful, and the promises given them of present assistance and future reward, we are plainly taught the high and responsible nature of this office. In the New Testament the rendering of respect and obedience to pastors and teachers is frequently insisted on as a Christian duty, and the dignity, as well as the indispensable utility, of the function is thus clearly recognized. "Obey them that have the rule over you, and submit yourselves; for they watch for your souls, as they that must give account, that they may do it with joy, and not with grief." "Let the elders that rule well be counted worthy of double honour, especially they who labour in the word and doctrine."

The experience of the Church in all ages amply confirms the clear intimations of Scripture, that, for the effective preaching of the Gospel, and the maintenance of the purity and peace of the Christian community, there is needed a well educated and thoroughly equipped ministry.

The erection of places of worship is also necessary in order that the people may be able to come together for the service of God and to wait on the ministrations of the word. Such edifices must necessarily differ widely in respect of size, form and costliness; but these principles may be gathered from Scripture and will receive general assent, that they should be sufficient in number and in capacity to meet the requirements of the whole population, and that both in external appearance and in the arrangements of the interior, there should be an avoidance of everything which either by its deformity or meanness, or by its extravagance and inappropriateness, might interfere with the devotions of the worshippers. In our large cities, the building of new churches is urgently required, and although there has been much noble Christian enterprise in this direction, there are few of those cities in which the provision of additional churches keeps pace with the constant increase of the population.

Missions to the heathen, to the Jews, and to countries in which Christian truth has been obscured by superstition or undermined by infidelity, next demand attention. And there is no truer index to the degree of vitality and strength existing in a church, than its active interest in the propagation of the faith which it professes among less favoured nations. Dr Max Müller has recently drawn attention to the fact, recognized long ago, that only missionary churches hold their ground in the march of progress. This is to be accounted for, not so much by referring to the tendency of such enterprise to react salutarily upon the church, as by considering that only a living and earnest church is moved to seek the lengthening of its cords and the strengthening of its stakes. A living church is of necessity a missionary church, and its field of operation is the world. The Kingdom of God is confined to no nationality, "Many shall come from the east and west, and shall sit down with Abraham, and Isaac, and Jacob, in the Kingdom of Heaven." Hundreds of millions of our fellowmen are even now sending up to heaven the inarticulate cry of the soul for light, and to the Church the stewardship of the light has been committed.

> "Shall we whose souls are lighted
> With wisdom from on high,
> Shall we to men benighted,
> The lamp of life deny?"

No! the sceptic and the man of the world may continue to make missionary operations the butt of their ridicule, but as long as the fire of holy love burns in the heart of the Church, and the light of truth illumines it, it will continue to be moved profoundly by the condition of the heathen, and to send forth labourers into those waiting fields to reap a harvest for Christ. It will seek to present every man perfect in Christ Jesus, and labour for this end, striving according to His working who works in it mightily.

After the Pulpit, and next in order as a means of evangelization, is the Press. During the last four hundred years the marvellous art associated in its origin with the names of Coster and Gutenberg has been revolutionising procedure in every sphere of human activity. The form of our literature, the character of our schools of learning, the methods of our trade and commerce, have all been altered by it. And the work of the Church has not been exempt from changes effected by the same potent spell. Instruction, for which the spoken address was formerly the only vehicle, is now conveyed more certainly, in a more permanent form, and to an immensely wider circle of disciples, by means of the printed book. The Bible, instead of being a rare and costly volume obtainable only by the very wealthy, can now be supplied in almost all the languages of the earth, and at a price which puts it within the reach of the poorest. The Press thus becomes the instrument of the Church. And every year sees its importance in this connection increasing. There are circles rarely or never accessible to the voice of the preacher, but the book finds it way into them. And while it may be true that, in respect of power to convince and move, no written or printed document can equal the voice of the sincere and earnest preacher, in other respects, and particularly in the scope which it affords for the elaborate treatment of the subject in hand, the palm must be assigned to the written book. But if the Press has furnished the Church with additional facilities for accomplishing its work it has also, alas! rendered similar assistance to the Church's foes. As we write, infidelity, superstition and vice are scattering their missives side by side with the Gospel of truth and holiness, and it is to be feared that in number and in the extent of their circulation, the vehicles of evil greatly surpass those of good. This is a matter which forces itself upon our attention with ever-increasing urgency. How to secure the Press for Christ? How to stay, or, if it be not possible to stay, how to counteract that pernicious literature, which like a flood of black and foul poison is deluging the land—this is a question than which few more deserve and demand our serious consideration.

With regard to Education, the opinion is prevailing more and more, that to provide it for those children whose parents are unable to provide it for them, belongs to the State; and the recent establishment of a national system has to some extent removed the necessity for the voluntary support of schools for secular instruction. There must always however be some cases, which the national provision does not overtake, and others in which government aid may with great advantage be supplemented by private benefactions. And the enlightened Christian will consider it his duty to take a lively and practical interest in the training and instruction of the young minds which are to constitute the strength for good or for evil of the next generation. "That the soul be without knowledge, it is not good," is the intimation of the Old Testament, and in the New we have many such admonitions as "Be not children in understanding;" "Add to your virtue knowledge." The maxim that Ignorance is the mother of Devotion, is worthy only of the Dark Ages, and of a religion which seeks to found itself upon the superstitious hopes and fears of the people. "Let there be Light," is the everlasting proclamation of Christ in the realm of the spiritual, as it was once his sublime *fiat* in the realm of the natural.

But supposing day schools erected in every necessitous district, and fully furnished with all appliances, the wants of Sunday schools are still to be supplied. The usefulness of Sunday schools has been variously appreciated; and they are no doubt much more urgently required, and much more useful, among some classes of the community than among others. But taking the lowest estimate of their value, they are centres of much good influence, especially among the children of the poor and the uneducated in our large cities and manufacturing districts. The Church is therefore under obligation to maintain and increase their efficiency, both by furnishing capable teachers and by providing all necessary funds.

Our next department of Christian work is one that presents greater difficulties. The poor, we are told, we shall always have with us; and by the same authority we are informed of our obligation to relieve their distresses and to supply their wants. It is held out by Paul as an inducement to diligence in honest labour, that thus a man will be enabled to give to those who are in need. If poverty were in all cases the result of uncontrollable causes, such as actual deficiency in the land of the food and raiment necessary to meet the requirements of the population, the duty of the Christian would be clear; but when, as in our own country, pauperism is the result chiefly of the frightful waste which pervades the social system,—waste of labour, waste of substance, waste of health, through ignorance and intemperance,—the question of duty is complicated. We have a recognition of the difficulty in the not less scholarly than sagacious rendering of Psalm xli. 1, by the authors of our metrical version,—" Blessed is he that *wisely* doth the poor man's case consider." To despise the poor is a sin, and one strongly denounced in Scripture; but it is not less a sin to pauperise those who might, if they would, support themselves with their hands, and the consequences in the latter case may be even more disastrous and may reach farther than in the former. To determine what constitutes poverty is somewhat difficult, as the question admits of every variety of answer. A bishop of the Church of England may, without deviating greatly from the style and mode of living conventionally prescribed to his order, find himself in straitened circumstances on his "miserable pittance of £4000 a year." Goldsmith towards the close of last century described the village preacher as "passing rich on forty pounds a year." Most persons experienced in collecting money, for religious or benevolent purposes, can tell of men worth hundreds of thousands of pounds, who habitually plead poverty as the excuse for withholding aid, or doling it out in infinitesimal quantities. And on the other hand there are multitudes of Christian men and women who, having learned, like the Apostle Paul, in whatsoever state they are therewith to be content, are really and truly rich in contentment and self-restraint, though their estate is "*nil*," and their income barely sufficient to procure the absolute necessaries of life. In the absence of any satisfactory definition of poverty, it may be worth while noticing a fact which cannot be better stated than in the words of an inspired observer, "I have been young and now am old, yet have I not seen the righteous forsaken, nor his seed begging bread." The good man is less likely to be found among the aid-seeking poor, both because his regulated and dutiful life, his industry and his prudence, tend to secure him a sufficiency, and because the limitation of his desires for the things of the world, and his interest in a treasure laid up in heaven, enable him to support with patience privations, under which another would murmur and complain. It is not assuredly from the ranks of the godly that the mighty host of our pauper population is mainly recruited. It follows that the indiscriminate or injudicious bestowal of alms on the humbler ranks of the people, whether from the public purse or by private individuals, is the occasion of gigantic and self-perpetuating evils. The pauperism of the United Kingdom is indeed appalling in its magnitude, and in the rapidity with which it increases. Nearly 1,500,000 of the population are in the receipt of aid from the Poors' Rates, and this in a country the richest in the world, at a period of unexampled commercial and manufacturing prosperity, and with wages high. But the expenditure of £130,000,000 yearly on intoxicating liquors, with the idleness, prodigality, waste and disease resulting from the excessive drinking of great numbers of the people, are the real causes of this deplorable state of things. The duty of the Church with regard to such a pauperism as disgraces our country, is *first* to seek to prevent it, and in the *second* place to seek the alleviation of the suffering it entails. In 1872 more than £12,000,000 of Police and Poors' Rates were expended in England and Wales alone. There cannot be a doubt that by far the larger portion of this outlay was indirectly an offering at the shrines of Intemperance and Vice. We do not pretend to make any complete statement of the position of this great and pressing question, still less to suggest any solution. But we maintain that what is required is, not the distribution of alms in larger amount from the pockets of ratepayers, but a thorough consideration of the causes in which the evil originates and the energetic employment of all means for their removal.

But no parochial-relief system that can be devised will ever overtake all the work delegated to Christian charity, so as to leave no room for kindly personal ministration by the rich to their poorer brethren. Indeed, if so desirable a result as the utter extinction of all spiritless, shiftless, and degraded pauperism were secured, this would only clear the way for a large-hearted and more magnificent charity, which would really bless both giver and receiver as being the offspring of sincere and considerate interest, and as not tending in any way to impair due self-respect in those on whom it was bestowed. Notwithstanding an opinion sometimes expressed to the contrary, the poor often stand far more in need of kindly interest, sympathy, and perhaps counsel, than of pecuniary assistance; and it is only when the gift is felt to be the outcome of real kindliness that it can be received without injury. Help tendered in a cold, official manner, whether by the public officer or from a private purse, is apt to do even more harm than good; whereas, when the hand bestowing is unmistakably moved by the promptings of a considerate mind and a loving heart, the self-respect of the recipient is rather increased than diminished by the communication. The time will come, and it is the duty of the Christian to anticipate it, when we shall recognise fully the duty of showing practical kindness to one another, and of carrying into the great family of the Church a larger portion of that spirit, and more of those gentle offices, which are seen to be so becoming in the smaller family of the household. Destitution may be made to cease from the land, but there will always be inequality of fortune as of position, some struggling with the *embarras de richesses*, others labouring under the commonplace burdens of toil and care. Either lot may be made a happy one, for it is in man himself more than in his circumstances that the conditions of happiness reside; but both rich and poor will assuredly be happier when relations of mutual respect and helpfulness exist between them, when poverty no longer shuts out the poor from the regards and sympathy of the rich, and when the unaffected kindliness of the rich precludes grudging or envy on the part of the poor.

There remain to be noticed as part of the machinery set in motion by Christian zeal for the accomplishment of good, such institutions as hospitals, infirmaries, and convalescent homes, asylums and refuges, and homes for fatherless and orphan children. These are indeed the glory of Christianity, for they have sprung directly from the example, the precepts, and the inspiration of Christ. A silent but mighty power has been exerted in the hidden recesses of the hearts and consciences of men by such parts of Scripture as the Parable of the Good Samaritan, and the account of the Judgment; and the results have been works which are the admiration of the world. Not only did our Lord take the weak, the suffering, and the neglected under His personal care when He was on the earth; He provided for them to all coming time. His words—"Inasmuch as ye have done it unto one of the least of these My brethren ye have done it unto Me,"—have yielded more even in money value than the cost of erecting and endowing a thousand hospitals. Secularism, whatever virtues it may lay claim to, cannot clear itself from the charge of selfishness. It has never done anything worthy of mention for the poor, the helpless, the sick, the widow or the orphan.

Such are the principal means by which the Church seeks to bring about that blessed change in the state and aspect of the world which its Founder rejoiced to contemplate from afar, and which He sacrificed His life to effect. All of them to be successful must be employed by sincere and loving hearts, directed by intelligence and wisdom, accompanied by prayer, and sustained by the gifts of the Christian people. It is the last of these conditions of their usefulness with which we are now specially concerned. Money, which when coveted, or hoarded, or squandered, is the occasion of so much evil, is required of us by God; and it is accepted by Him, when given by grateful and loyal hearts, as a pleasing sacrifice and a sweet-smelling savour. He, whom it pleased to save man by the foolishness of preaching, has also seen it meet to make the dedication of money to His service a means of grace to the giver and a means of spiritual blessing to the world. It is not that to the silver and the gold in themselves, or to the things they represent, any spiritual force has been communicated. It is not that He, to whom the world and all things in it belong, cannot dispense with them in the working out of His purposes. It is not that all the wealth of the world could for a moment be balanced against the worth of one human soul. Those who give most readily and most liberally are perhaps the most deeply sensible of the inferiority of the material to the spiritual, and of the utter insufficiency of merely material forces to achieve spiritual ends. But giving to God at once expresses and fosters a spirit of prayer, of consecration, and of self-denial, from which proceed ever-accumulating results, the ultimate grandeur of which it is impossible to forecast.

It would be out of place to attempt here any justification of God's way in this matter, but we may merely refer to this, that it puts it within the power of every Christian to take part in the works which have been enumerated. All cannot be preachers of the Gospel, or writers for the press in its interests. Everyone cannot build a church or school, or endow an hospital; but by giving of his means, every one may take a real and substantial part in all these works.

Looked at in the true light, the giving of money for these purposes is a laying it at the feet of Christ. The contribution made to any worthy object in the name of Christ is precious in His sight, and takes its place with the gifts of the Magi, and with the precious ointment with which Mary anointed His feet. In this light, the Christian should consider all his giving; the silver and the gold should be lost sight of, and attention fixed on what they represent—the gratitude of the heart in bestowing them, the joy of Christ in receiving them, and the universal blessedness which they are helping on. Only let the place and power of money in the Christian dispensation be understood and kept in view, and there will be no danger of the Church being either crippled in its operations by want of funds, or secularised by the schemes set on foot to provide them. There will then be universal, cheerful, and constant giving, and the only limits to the amounts contributed will be that set by the amounts required.

Come then, Christians, in the spirit of your Master, with faith in His teaching, with trust in His promises, and with the love of a redeemed heart to its Redeemer, and to all who are or may be His, burning within you, come to this blessed exchange to which He graciously invites you! "Make to yourselves friends of the mammon of unrighteousness. Sell that ye have and give alms; provide yourselves bags which wax not old, a treasure in the heavens which faileth not." Barter the perishable riches of this world for the substantial and enduring glories of that Kingdom of God which shall yet extend "from sea to sea, and from the river unto the ends of the earth."

CHAPTER III.

THE SCRIPTURE ACCOUNT OF THE DUTY OF GIVING TO GOD.

However strongly a particular line of action may be approved by our Christian consciousness and common sense, and however much may be adduced in its favour from the tradition of the Fathers and the established usages of the Church, it is generally felt that before it can claim to be binding on the conscience and heart of Christians, it must produce the authority of Scripture. There is a not unreasonable hesitation in many minds to accept of theories or methods in religion, however promising, until they are shown to be stamped with the approval of that wisdom which is higher than man's. To the law and to the testimony, therefore, we propose now to appeal. What saith the Scripture concerning the duty of giving? The answers are so numerous and so various in form, though all to the same effect, that our difficulty will be rather in selecting than in finding. Indeed, those whose attention has not been given to this subject, and who complacently cherish the opinion that a theoretical acceptance of the Gospel, and conformity more or less exact to the moral law as expressed in the decalogue, constitute the whole duty of man, and that giving to the Church, to missions, and to the poor is a work of supererogation rather than obedience to an absolute divine requirement, might well be startled could they have brought before them in one view all the Bible utterances respecting this duty, its explicit declarations, its strong reasons, its urgent appeals, its pathetic entreaties, its solemn warnings. It is impossible to peruse these, with unbiassed mind, without being forced to the conclusion that giving to God is an integral part of religious service, and that it is our duty diligently to concentrate attention upon it, in order that it may be rendered in the form that is most in accordance with the divine will.

Classifying these utterances, we find that those which bear upon the nature and obligatoriness of the duty, set it before us as being at once an act of worship, a token of gratitude to God, an expression of interest in our fellowmen, a means of grace to ourselves, and a condition of temporal prosperity. Instructions relative to the mode of performance enjoin upon us to engage in it intelligently, liberally, systematically, with promptitude and cheerfully. The space at our command does not admit of our adducing many quotations in support of these positions, and a few will suffice to establish them.

1. *Giving, an act of worship.*—The worship of God in spirit and the presentation of gifts upon His altar, were associated from the earliest times. Abel offered of his flocks, Cain of the fruit of the ground. The patriarchal dispensation has its records of liberal and faithful consecration of property to God. The Mosaic economy was characterised by the number and minuteness of the directions given to the people for their guidance in offering to Jehovah a set portion of the substance with which He had enriched them. We find the offering, tithe, or gift everywhere required and rendered as an acknowledgment of the divine sovereignty and universal proprietorship. This is conspicuously and beautifully seen in the account given of the offerings for the erection of the temple, and in David's prayer on that occasion. We are told of the enthusiasm by which all were animated. The chief of the fathers and princes of

Israel, and the captains of thousands and of hundreds, with the rulers over the king's work, offered willingly, and gave for the service of the house of God. The sublime words of David's prayer reveal the spirit which actuated the people, and the motives which determined their gifts, "Thine, O Lord, is the greatness, and the power, and the glory, and the victory, and the majesty: for all that is in the heaven and the earth is Thine: Thine is the kingdom, O Lord, and Thou art exalted as head above all. Both riches and honour come of Thee, and Thou reignest over all: and in Thine hand is power and might: and in Thine hand it is to make great and to give strength unto all. Now, therefore, our God, we thank Thee, and praise Thy glorious name. But who am I, and what is my people, that we should be able to offer so willingly after this sort? for all things come of Thee, and of Thine own have we given Thee."

The existence of a divine proprietorship in the earth, superior to that of tenant, lord, or king, is strongly insisted on; and along with the assertions of this proprietorship we find invocations to bring the homage of the heart and offerings of substance. "The earth is the Lord's and the fulness thereof." "All the earth is Mine." "Every tree of the forest is Mine, and the cattle upon a thousand hills." "The silver is Mine and the gold is Mine," saith the Lord of hosts. "Give unto the Lord, O ye kindreds of the people, give unto the Lord glory and strength. Give unto the Lord the glory due unto His name; bring an offering, and come into His courts. O worship the Lord in the beauty of holiness." "Vow, and pay unto the Lord your God. Let all that be round about Him bring presents unto Him that ought to be feared." God the Maker and Sustainer of all, requiring us thus to acknowledge Him by giving to Him of His own, we have before us a sacred duty, resting on no questionable foundation of human wisdom, but on the indisputable, "Thus saith the Lord."

The evidence of the prophetical writings concurs to establish this conclusion. In the course of delineating the future glory of the earth, when it shall have been subdued by Christ, David tells how the gifts of God's people will then flow into His treasury. "They that dwell in the wilderness shall bow before Him; and His enemies shall lick the dust. The kings of Tarshish and of the isles shall bring presents: the kings of Sheba and Seba shall offer gifts." And in that day we are assured, that "the vile person shall no more be called liberal, nor the churl said to be bountiful."

Still further confirmation is afforded by the denunciation of those who sinned in withholding the offerings required by the law. The prophet Malachi was instructed thus to address the people at a time of general declension, "Will a man rob God? yet ye have robbed Me. Ye are cursed with a curse, for ye have robbed Me, even this whole nation." "Ye said also, Behold, what a weariness is it? and ye have snuffed at it, saith the Lord of hosts; and ye brought that which was torn, and the lame, and the sick; thus ye brought an offering: should I accept this of your hand? saith the Lord. But cursed be the deceiver, which hath in his flock a male, and voweth, and sacrificeth unto the Lord a corrupt thing; for I am a great King, saith the Lord of hosts, and My name is dreadful among the heathen."

2. *Giving, a token of gratitude to God.*—" What shall I render unto the Lord for all His benefits towards me?" asks the Psalmist, and he himself declares his resolution, "I will take the cup of salvation,

and call upon the name of the Lord. I will pay my vows unto the Lord now in the presence of all His people." Over and above the tithes required by the law, the people were encouraged to present freewill offerings as an acknowledgment of the divine goodness on extraordinary occasions, and many instances of their doing so are recorded with approbation. The great commandment, "Thou shalt love the Lord thy God with all thy heart, and with all thy soul, and with all thy mind," requires of us a disposition which, wherever it exists, will find its expression in some tangible form. The love to God that seeks no expression is a pretence. That which is fitful in its manifestations has a constant tendency to grow feeble and cold. It is true that those love much who have been forgiven much, but it is no less true that those love much who unweariedly seek and find channels in which the stream of their love may flow. Christ recognised this truth when He sent those whom He had healed to offer the customary gift in the temple. And the Apostle Paul, while urging upon the Corinthians a diligent cultivation of the grace of charity, in ministering to the poor, adds this as an additional incentive, "For the administration of this service not only supplieth the want of the saints, but is abundant also by many thanksgivings unto God." The Christian of these days is a recipient of divine bounty in larger measure than was the Jew in olden times, and his obligations are correspondingly increased. Much has been given to him, and much is due from him. Paul places this in a clear light, "The love of Christ constraineth us; because we thus judge, that if one died for all, then were all dead; and that He died for all, that they which live should not henceforth live unto themselves, but unto Him which died for them, and rose again." It is indeed a small thing, that those who have been blessed with all spiritual blessings in heavenly places in Christ, should give of their carnal things as an acknowledgment of His goodness. Body, soul, and spirit are to be wholly consecrated to Christ, how much more the possessions of His people. If He has so loved us as to give Himself for us, can any expression of gratitude be too costly? In the gospels we have the divine approval of a gift of gratitude, which was pronounced by contemporary opinion extravagant, and a proof of infatuation. Nothing could be more instructive than the touching representation of Mary after the anointing of Jesus' feet, shrinking under the angry reproof of the wise and prudent ones, to whom her deed of love had seemed an act of sinful waste, but reassured and gladdened by the gracious words of Christ, "Let her alone, why trouble ye her, she hath wrought a good work upon Me." And how fitted to overwhelm with shame were the words addressed to one of those thinkers of evil, "Simon, seest thou this woman? I entered into thine house, thou gavest Me no water for my feet: but she hath washed My feet with tears, and wiped them with the hairs of her head. Thou gavest Me no kiss: but this woman since the time I came in hath not ceased to kiss My feet. My head with oil thou didst not anoint: but this woman hath anointed My feet with ointment."

3. *Giving, an expression of interest in our fellows.* Under the old economy the claims of the poor, the weak and the helpless, on the benevolence of the community, were distinctly recognized, and ample provision was made for meeting them. God identified himself with the poor in order to encourage the shewing of kindness to them. "He that hath pity upon the poor lendeth to the Lord." Among other characteristics of the good man

his philanthropy is dwelt upon. "When the ear heard me, then it blessed me; and when the eye saw me, it gave witness to me: because I delivered the poor that cried, and the fatherless, and him that had none to help him. The blessing of him that was ready to perish came upon me: and I caused the widow's heart to sing for joy." And in reproving the people for the godlessness of their lives notwithstanding great professions of spirituality, God calls upon them to prove the sincerity of their faith by deeds of charity. "Is not this the fast that I have chosen? to loose the bands of wickedness, to undo the heavy burdens, and to let the oppressed go free, and that ye break every yoke. Is it not to deal thy bread to the hungry, and that thou bring the poor that are cast out to thy house? when thou seest the naked, that thou cover him and that thou hide not thyself from thine own flesh?"

But it is in the New Testament with its larger and brighter hope, and its more catholic spirit, that we find the most earnest persuasives to giving, as a means of securing the good of our fellows. Here we breathe an atmosphere full of love and of the spirit of sacrifice. "Beloved, if God so loved us, we ought also to love one another," is the argument which it addresses to the heart of the Christian. And how clearly is it shown that the natural outcome of this love is in kindly deeds and in cheerful sacrifice for others. "To do good and to communicate, forget not." "I have shown you how that so labouring ye ought to support the weak, and to remember the words of the Lord Jesus, how He said, It is more blessed to give than to receive." How pitilessly is the veil torn from that pretentious pietism which acknowledges no obligations of this kind. "Whoso hath this world's good, and seeth his brother have need, and shutteth up his bowels of compassion from him, how dwelleth the love of God in him?" The profession of Christianity when it is not accompanied by a readiness to part with personal comforts and advantages for the sake of others is indeed a miserable hypocrisy, a libel on the religion of Him who out of His own experience taught that it is more blessed to give than to receive, and who Himself, though He was rich, yet for our sakes became poor, that through His poverty we might be rich. How much of true blessedness the Church fails to experience, how often it is weak when it might be strong, and ashamed when it should be speaking with its enemies in the gate, because of its failure to recognise the duty of following in its Lord's steps and of manifesting the same sincere and disinterested love to men which was shown in His self-denial and sacrifice! There was a time when the Church was so poor, that one of its leaders was found saying, "Silver and gold have I none." But, oh how warm the heart of the Church was then, how lively its sympathies, how bright its hope, how enduring its patience! Would that the old spirit were revived! Then many a treasure which is not only in danger of becoming corrupt and cankered itself, but threatens to corrupt the heart of its possessor, would be brought forth, to be laid at the feet of Jesus, and to be applied in promoting the temporal and spiritual well-being of those whom He is not ashamed to call His brethren.

4. *Giving, a means of grace to the giver.* All honest work reacts on the doer, increasing power and elevating character; and the same holds good of giving. The gift which ministers to the carrying on of some good work is at the same time the occasion of spiritual blessing to the bestower. This is clearly and frequently

taught in the Scriptures. In that passage from Isaiah already quoted, in which the claims of the hungry, the poor and the naked are pleaded, this magnificent promise is made to those who shall respond to them, "Then shall thy light break forth as the morning, and thine health shall spring forth speedily: and thy righteousness shall go before thee; the glory of the Lord shall be thy rearward. And if thou draw out thy soul to the hungry and satisfy the afflicted soul; then shall thy light rise in obscurity, and thy darkness be as the noonday, and the Lord shall guide thee continually." In the teaching of Christ, this truth is often conveyed under the allegory of a market transaction. Those who part with worldly wealth for His sake receive, in exchange, He tells us, the treasures of heaven. "Sell all that thou hast," He said to the young ruler, "and distribute unto the poor, and thou shalt have treasure in heaven." The words, "Whosoever he be of you that forsaketh not all that he hath, he cannot be My disciple," have been a stumbling-block to many. We do not suppose that Christ requires all who would follow Him to divest themselves of their property, as the condition of being enrolled among his disciples. So far from a wholesale repudiation of property by Christians being beneficial, it would be disastrous both to the Church and to society. But it is clear from this and similar statements, that readiness to part with all at the Master's command is required. And when He has seen meet to utter this command, and His people have loyally responded to it, then the benignity concealed in the apparent harshness has been abundantly manifested. The pain of parting, the sharp agony, sly loss, have been succeeded by a rush of heavenly peich and joy upon the soul as the nearness of Chriath presence has been realised. The chambers of the h and having been vacated by the noisy troop of cares and pleasures of earth, Christ has entered in and filled them with a glorious company of heavenly thoughts and hopes. Impoverished in the estimation of the world, they have been made truly rich. Deprived of that portion of the world's goods which they once called their own, they have obtained a surer title to the inheritance of the whole, for the meek alone truly inherit the earth. Christ's declaration is found by them to be already receiving its fulfilment in their experience,—" Every one that hath forsaken houses, or brethren, or sisters, or father, or mother, or wife, or children, or lands, for My name's sake, shall receive an hundredfold, and shall inherit everlasting life."

On the other hand, the Scriptures abound in warnings against the sin of exclusive devotion to selfish interests, and in representations of the terrible loss which the soul sustains, when no place is found in it for the generous emotions. " Charge them that are rich in this world, that they be not high-minded, nor trust in uncertain riches, but in the living God, who giveth us richly all things to enjoy: that they do good, that they be rich in good works, ready to distribute, willing to communicate: laying up in store for themselves a good foundation against the time to come, that they may lay hold on eternal life." " Let not the rich man glory in his riches; but let him that glorieth glory in this, that he understandeth and knoweth Me, that I am the Lord, which exercise loving-kindness, judgment, and righteousness in the earth: for in these things I delight, saith the

1. Christ himself in many ways sought to impress *giving* he rich that much diligence was needful on their gift is i they would preserve their freedom and integrity. the give ardly shall they that have riches enter into the

Kingdom of Heaven," He was wont to observe. In the parable of the Sower, the thorns which grew up and choked the good seed were the cares of the world and the deceitfulness of riches. "Woe unto you that are rich!" He exclaimed, on another occasion, as much in sorrow as in anger, "for ye have received your consolation. Woe unto you that are full! for ye shall hunger. Woe unto you that laugh now! for ye shall mourn and weep." The only way in which the rich can effectually guard against the dangers of worldliness, forgetfulness of God, and selfish isolation, to which they are exposed, is by constantly bearing in mind their true position, as being merely stewards of God's bounties and as being under obligations therefore so to lay out His trust that when it is required again at their hands, they may be able to render an account of it with joy.

5. *Giving, a condition of temporal prosperity.* Under the old dispensation promises of temporal good, as the reward of obedience and devotion, were held out very freely, and the new by no means excludes them. We are nowhere indeed encouraged to make such good an end, and to act rightly only in order to secure it. But it is intimated that God's government of the world is in the interest of those who seek to do His will, and that He will honour those who thus honour Him. To this effect are such passages as the following:—"Honour the Lord with thy substance, and with the first-fruits of all thine increase: so shall thy barns be filled with plenty, and thy presses shall burst out with new wine." "There is that scattereth and yet increaseth; and there is that withholdeth more than is meet, but it tendeth to poverty." "The liberal soul shall be made fat." "He which soweth sparingly shall reap also sparingly; and he which soweth bountifully shall reap also bountifully; and

"Give, and it shall be given unto you; good measure, pressed down, and shaken together, and running over, shall men give into your bosom. For with the same measure that ye mete withal it shall be measured to you again." "He that hath pity upon the poor, lendeth unto the Lord, and that which he hath given will He pay him again." "Bring ye all the tithes into the storehouse, that there may be meat in Mine house, and prove Me now herewith, saith the Lord of Hosts, if I will not open you the windows of heaven, and pour you out a blessing, that there shall not be room enough to receive it." These and a multitude of similar declarations all tend to the establishment of the conclusion, which experience amply confirms, that those who give liberally of their substance to the cause of God and of their fellow-men, receive more even in the form of earthly increase than they thus expend, and that he who would be the successful husbandman, or merchant, or manufacturer, does wisely even from a worldly point of view when he adopts a policy of large-heartedness and munificence.

We have thus set forth, in order, a few of the many Scripture statements bearing on the nature and obligatoriness of this duty. But there are other passages, the testimony of which, to the existence of the obligation, is still stronger, as it is of the indirect kind; passages in which the duty itself being taken for granted, we are told how it should be performed. To some of these we would draw attention, and the whole scope of Scripture teaching on this important subject will then be before us.

1. *The Scriptures enjoin intelligent and devout giving.* We are not to suppose that the offering of a gift is in itself, and apart from the views and motives of the giver, necessarily pleasing to God. On the contrary,

giving even to the cause of God may be a sin in the giver, the manner being impious, or the motives impure. Saul on one occasion offered burnt-offerings and peace-offerings to God. Both of these were appointed by the law, and, had they been offered by one invested with the priestly office, they would doubtless have been accepted. But Saul's assumption of that office was a usurpation, and, instead of propitiating the favour of God, his proffered gift only provoked the reproof, "Thou hast done foolishly : thou hast not kept the commandment of the Lord thy God." A similar case is recorded in the New Testament, that of Simon Magus, who offered money to the apostles as an inducement to them to confer on him the power of communicating the Holy Ghost. His offering being prompted by covetousness, was rejected in these indignant words, "Thy money perish with thee, because thou hast thought that the gift of God may be purchased with money." The prophets were frequently commanded to intimate to the people the rejection of their gifts, because of the impure motives, or the inconsistent lives, of those who brought them. "To what purpose is the multitude of your sacrifices unto me," asks God by the mouth of Isaiah, "I am full of the burnt-offerings of rams, and the fat of fed beasts ; and I delight not in the blood of bullocks, or of lambs, or of he-goats. Bring no more vain oblations; incense is an abomination unto Me." And then the reason why those observances which He Himself had appointed had become displeasing, is stated, —" Your hands are full of blood."

The principle of devout acceptable giving is well stated by Paul in the commendation which he passes on the churches of Macedonia for their liberality. In speaking of them he says, "They first gave their own selves to the Lord, and unto us by the will of God;" and then adds, "To their power, I bear record, yea and beyond their power, they were willing of themselves" to minister to the saints. The careful avoidance of ostentation in giving is recommended both in the exhortation of Paul, "He that giveth let him do it with simplicity," and in the still more forcible precept of Christ, "Let not thy left hand know what thy right hand doeth."

2. *The Scriptures enjoin liberal giving.* Those whose immediate inquiry on encountering any of the claims which God has upon their means is, how little can I give, must have either failed to observe, or, what is more probable, failed to profit by much of the teaching of God's Word. The first of all the fruits of the field and the produce of the cattle were claimed by God from Israel, and nothing imperfect or blemished was to be laid upon His altar. All the materials employed in the construction, first of the tabernacle and afterwards of the temple, were the finest and most costly of their kind. Gold and silver in profusion adorned them both. Nothing was too good or too valuable to be employed in this service. And the demands of the Gospel are even larger than those of the law. "Freely ye have received, freely give." It has been the opinion of many able commentators and antiquarians that, according to the law, a Jew was under obligation to devote from two-fifths to one-third of his entire income to religious and charitable purposes. The early Christians we know far exceeded this proportion in their liberality, many of them selling all that they possessed in order that they might have to give to their poorer neighbours in a time of pressing need.

3. *The Scriptures enjoin systematic giving.* We shall afterwards more fully consider the light which the

Scriptures throw on the question as to what proportion offerings should bear to income. At present we desire merely to draw attention to the care with which amounts and proportions are recorded from the very first. From the record of the giving of tithes by Abraham to Melchizedek, down to the mention of the two mites offered by the widow in the temple, we have a continuous line of statistics. What, for example, could be more systematic than the payment of tithes as prescribed and regulated by the Mosaic law? And it is important to observe that our Lord, in whose teaching the protesting and revolutionising elements so often prevailed, directly expressed His approval of scrupulous exactness in this matter. When reproving the Pharisees for the inconsistency of nicely estimating the tithes of mint, anise, and cummin due by them, and neglecting the weightier matters of the law, judgment, mercy, and faith, He added, "These ought ye to have done, *and not to leave the other undone.*"

4. *The Scriptures enjoin promptitude in giving.* "Whatsoever thy hand findeth to do, do it with thy might; for there is no work, nor device, nor knowledge, nor wisdom in the grave whither thou goest." This counsel of the Wise Man applies to giving as to all other duties. "When thou shalt vow a vow unto the Lord thy God, thou shalt not be slack to pay it." Say not to thy neighbour, "Go and come again, when thou hast it by thee." It is interesting to observe Paul's recommendation of promptitude as well as liberality to the Corinthians, "Herein I give my advice, for this is expedient for you, who have begun before, not only to do, but also to be forward a year ago. *Now, therefore, perform the doing of it;* that as there was a readiness to will, so there may be a performance also out of that

which ye have." "I thought it necessary to exhort the brethren that they would go before unto you, and make up beforehand your bounty whereof ye had notice before *that the same might be ready.*" An opinion is too commonly entertained that irregularity, such as would not be tolerated in the discharge of obligations between man and man, is quite admissible in the service of Christ, and that Christians may withhold their offerings, or diminish them, or present them carelessly and fitfully, without incurring blame. But in opposition to this opinion, may be presented such words as these, "When thou vowest a vow unto the Lord, defer not to pay it; for He hath no pleasure in fools: pay that which thou hast vowed." In full accord with these express commands, is the spirit of all enactments relating to the subject, and of all historical statements illustrative of it. The whole testimony forces upon us the conclusion, that if regularity and promptitude are admirable and desirable qualities in the transaction of ordinary business, we are bound to cultivate them in connection with the service of God.

5. *The Scriptures enjoin cheerful giving.* Even under the dispensation of positive commands, much importance was attached to willinghood. "Speak unto the Children of Israel that they bring Me an offering: of every man that giveth it willingly with his heart, shall ye take My offering." The historian, concluding his account of the lavish offerings of the people for the erection of the temple, says that "the people rejoiced, for that they offered willingly, because with perfect heart they offered willingly to the Lord." And Paul would rather have a smaller gift presented with cheerfulness than a large one given grudgingly. "Every man according as he purposeth in his heart, so let him give; not

grudgingly, or of necessity, for God loveth a cheerful giver." All service of God, when rightly engaged in, is joyful, and there is a peculiar joy with which God fills the hearts of those who are emptying themselves of earthly good in order that His kingdom may be advanced. Special mention is made of the joy of Israel at the dedication of the temple by Solomon, and at the dedication of the wall of Jerusalem by Nehemiah. On the latter occasion, we read that "Also that day, they offered great sacrifices, and rejoiced; for God had made them rejoice with great joy: the wives also and the children rejoiced; so that the joy of Jerusalem was heard even afar off."

Such is the conspicuous position assigned to the service of giving in the Word of God, the character with which it is invested, the manner in which the godly are required to render it. Is there not much in this teaching of Scripture which the Church of to-day has need to lay to heart? With all our boasted munificence in religious enterprise and in works of charity, will either the character or the amount of our liberality bear to have applied to them the divine standards of truth and duty?

CHAPTER IV.

SCRIPTURE ILLUSTRATONS OF THE DUTY.

IN the preceding chapter, we have presented chiefly, though not exclusively, precepts and intimations of a general character. We now proceed to consider what may be called the historical evidence furnished by Scripture in favour of systematic, proportionate, and frequent contributions for religious and benevolent purposes. In this matter, as in all others, the Bible instructs us both by laying down precept upon precept, line upon line, and by setting forth more or less fully the noble examples of obedience set by men of eminent wisdom and godliness, along with the happy results to themselves and their families of such a course. As civilization advances, and education improves the popular mind, teaching by concrete representation gives place more and more to appeals directed to the understanding and the reason; but as long as human nature retains its present characteristics, the consideration of an admirable example will more powerfully influence the mind, and more readily awaken enthusiasm, than any abstract considerations of duty unaccompanied by such enforcement. In any inquiry of this kind, therefore, it is proper besides asking—What saith the Scripture? to ask, What was the practice of the men whose lives are recorded in the Scripture as having been well-pleasing to God? and this is what we propose to do in the present chapter.

The first mention of systematic giving occurs in the history of Abraham, on the occasion of his victory over the four kings. On his return laden with the spoils of war, he was met by Melchizedek, King of Salem, priest of the Most High God, and having received the blessing of this illustrious personage, he presented to him a tenth part of all. It is extremely improbable that the custom of dedicating a tenth was originated by Abraham. The existence of such a custom among many Gentile nations, and in particular among the Greeks and Romans, who were accustomed to devote a tenth of their substance to the gods, makes it probable that it had its origin at the earliest period in the history of the race. The bareness of the record in the case of Abraham, and the absence of comment, favour the supposition that he was only acting in accordance with a custom already established. The authority of his example is of the highest order when we consider how singularly favoured he was by God. The designation Friend of God was applied to him, and a blessing was pronounced upon him unparalleled in its greatness and its far-reaching effect.

The example of Jacob is the next submitted to us, and it is one of much interest. The young man had just left his father's home under circumstances which quite precluded his return in peace. He was in the wilderness, alone, friendless and destitute; but even then he resolved that through life, in poverty or in wealth, he would give systematically to God. The proportion which he fixed upon was a tenth of his increase, and he solemnly vowed accordingly;—"This stone which I have set for a pillar shall be God's house; and of all that Thou shalt give me I will surely give the tenth unto Thee." How greatly Jacob prospered we learn from the subsequent history, and from his own words many years after when acknowledging the goodness of God—"I am not worthy of the least of all the mercies, and of all the truth, which Thou hast showed unto Thy servant; for with my staff I passed over this Jordan, and now I am become two bands."

The practice of proportionate giving which the Patriarchs had adopted, either voluntarily, or in accordance with prevalent custom, was made law for the Jews under the Mosaic economy, the proportion being at the same time increased. "All the tithe of the land, whether of the seed of the land or of the fruit of the tree, is the Lord's; it is holy unto the Lord." In addition to the tithe which was devoted to the support of the priestly tribe of Levi, there were other legal requirements for the service of the sanctuary and for the poor. The amount and frequency of these contributions are somewhat obscure, but they are commonly estimated to have been equivalent to a second tenth. And over and above all that was given in answer to the demands of the law, the people were encouraged, as we have already seen, to present free-will offerings on many special occasions, as tokens of gratitude for divine mercies.

These were the ordinary contributions of the people from day to day and from year to year. The regulations determining them formed an integral part of the Law. They were as binding on the conscience of the devout Jew as the requirements and the prohibitions of the Decalogue. They share the admiration and reverence which are so often expressed by the Psalmists. "Oh how love I thy law, it is my meditation all the day." "I understand more than the ancients, because I keep thy precepts." We know that just as these and other precepts of the law were obeyed, the people prospered; and that with neglect and disobedience there came the waste and ruin of war, and subjection to the rod of the oppressor. We know that after long periods of desertion and desolation, the first symptom of returning favour was an inquiry after the old paths and a determination to walk in them once more; and that every record of national contrition and renewal of obedience ushers in the history of brighter days and returning strength. Not more closely did the fortune of war in the conflict between Israel and Moab follow the uplifting or the falling of the hands of the man of God, than did the independence, the wealth, the glory of the Jewish people stand in relation to the degree of their faith in God and their obedience to His law.

That the zeal and joyous willingness of the people were not exhausted by these claims upon their substance was abundantly evident when any great work for which special preparation had to be made was undertaken. Such works were the erection of the Tabernacle, and the collection by David of material for the construction of the first temple. The pages that tell of the liberality and zeal of the Jewish people on these occasions must always be to the nation a source of pride, and no great or arduous work involving a necessity for much self-denial will ever be undertaken by the Church, without its recurring to those splendid examples. Let us glance at what took place when the tabernacle was to be reared. The command of God addressed through Moses gave the first impulse. "Take ye from among you an offering unto the Lord, whosoever is of a willing heart, let him bring it, an offering of the Lord." Then followed an intimation of the various materials required, that each might bring such as he possessed. The word had no sooner spread than the people proceeded without hesitation to bring in their gold, and silver, and brass; their cloth and wood and oil. "They came, every one whose heart stirred him up, and every one whom his spirit made willing, and they brought the Lord's offering to the work of the tabernacle of the congregation." "And they came, both men and women, as many as were willing-hearted, and brought bracelets, and earrings, and rings, and tablets, all jewels of gold; and every man that offered, offered an offering of gold unto the Lord." Those who had no jewellery brought the produce of their labour; the rulers brought onyx stones for the ephod and the breastplate; others came laden with spices, and oil for the light. Every one took part in the joyful sacrifice of that great day. The results were an overflowing treasury and fully-stocked workshops. "And all the wise men that wrought all the work of the sanctuary, came every man from his work which they made; and they spake unto Moses saying—

The people bring much more than enough for the service of the work which the Lord commanded to make. And Moses gave commandment, and they caused it to be proclaimed throughout the camp, saying, Let neither man nor woman make any more work for the offering of the sanctuary. So the people were restrained from bringing." How impressive is the lesson conveyed by the sequel of the narrative—" So Moses finished the work. Then a cloud covered the tent of the congregation:" and "the cloud abode thereon, and the glory of the Lord filled the tabernacle." These were days of glory and strength to Israel, and in them were laid the deep foundations of all her future greatness. They were days fragrant with blissful memories. The prophet Jeremiah touchingly alludes to them—"Thus saith the Lord; I remember thee, the kindness of thy youth, the love of thine espousals, when thou wentest after Me in the wilderness, in a land that was not sown. Israel was holiness unto the Lord, and the first fruits of his increase."

About four hundred years later, the Israelites having meanwhile entered the land of Canaan and established themselves in it, a pious purpose was formed in the heart of King David to build a house for the safe-keeping of the ark and for the worship of God. The work as planned by him (for God did not permit him to execute it) was of stupendous proportions, and his own labours and gifts were commensurately great. It has been calculated that the royal contributions alone amounted to about eighteen millions sterling. Such zeal in the monarch awakened a corresponding enthusiasm in the people. Having summoned the great congregation, and submitted to them his purpose, his plans and his preparations, the king concluded by asking, "Who then is willing to consecrate his service this day unto the

Lord?" At once there came back the hearty response, "We are willing," and at once great and small, the fathers, the princes, the captains of thousands and of hundreds, the rulers of the king's work and the common people, vied with each other in offerings of gold, silver, precious stones and other requisites. The heart of the good old king overflowed with joy, and all Israel rejoiced with him. A deep solemnity then fell upon the vast multitude, as from the royal lips there arose that sublime prayer for the kingdom and for Solomon, in which we trace the promise of the greatness and glory of the succeeding reign.

Other instances might be adduced from the Old Testament, and the book of Psalms in particular might be made to furnish many testimonies to the zeal and liberality in giving, displayed by good men under the old economy. But our space is limited, and we must now pass to the New Testament. Here on the very threshhold we encounter an act of giving associated with worship, the offering of gifts by the Magi to the Child Jesus. Did not the acceptance of these seal the character of the new worship as one in which giving was to be as essential a feature as it had been in the old. The presentation of the infant Redeemer in the temple was attended by the offering prescribed in the law of Moses. Our Lord himself from first to last of His ministry upheld the authority of the law in all matters of this nature, only protesting against the misconstructions and perversions of it by its professed expounders. He discountenanced the offering of a gift to God, while enmity to a brother filled the heart, but He would not have the gift carried away again. He would have it left before the altar, and the offended brother having been reconciled, He would then have the gift devoutly offered. He commanded those whom He cleansed to carry the appointed thankoffering to the priests. He miraculously provided for the payment of the temple tax by Himself and Peter. "The Scribes and Pharisees sit in Moses' seat," said He to the people;—"All therefore whatsoever they bid you observe, that observe and do." In some respects indeed, the teaching of the law was supplemented by Him. In particular, the acceptability of gifts in proportion to the extent of the self-denial involved, was impressively taught by a comparison which He instituted between the two mites cast into the treasury by a poor widow, and the much larger gifts deposited by wealthy men. "Of a truth," He said to His disciples, " this poor woman hath cast in more than they all, for all these have of their abundance cast in unto the offerings of God, but she of her penury, hath cast in all the living that she had." As to amount, the requirements of Christ sometimes greatly exceeded those of Moses. When He called His disciples for example, He bade them leave all and follow Him. The abandonment of property or profitable occupation at God's call, is just as truly an offering to God as the casting of money into the treasury. And this He required of His disciples. Their homes, their families, the nets by which they gained their livelihood, all were to be offered up as a sacrifice on the altar of faith and devotion. "Whosoever he be of you that forsaketh not all that he hath, he cannot be My disciple." We have reason to believe that many made such sacrifices. We are told of one individual on whom the influence of Christ's teaching was such, that he gave the half of his goods to the poor, besides making fourfold restitution to those whom at a former period he had defrauded. And the sincere repentance and hearty purpose of obedience evinced by this conduct drew from

Christ the congratulation, "This day is salvation come to this house, forasmuch as he also is a son of Abraham." On another occasion, a rich ruler came to Him, professing a desire to be instructed in the way of life. Christ pointed him to the moral law, but he speedily replied that he had carefully observed all its requirements. This was virtually to ask the question, What duty comes next in order? and Christ answered it by bidding him go and sell all that he had and distribute to the poor, assuring him that he would thus have treasure in heaven. This counsel was not accepted. It implied a heroism to which the faith and ardour of the inquirer were not equal. But it does not the less afford us an insight into the mind of Christ on this duty. We have already had occasion to remark that we are not to conclude, from Christ's having imposed such conditions on some of His followers, that it is the duty of every one to part with the whole of his property. The Christian capitalist employs his Lord's talents to much greater advantage, when he invests his wealth in some useful business, affording occupation and livelihood to many, than if he were to dissipate it in a thousand small charities. But we are led to conclude from this and other incidents, that Christ does require in those who would follow Him, a recognition of the incomparable superiority of the claims which the kingdom of God has upon men, over those of the most boundless wealth or the loftiest rank. There must be such an appreciation of the worth of the one thing needful, as to make it possible and even pleasant to part with all, if such sacrifice be necessary in order to secure or to retain it.

The teaching of Christ did not take full effect till after His death, or rather it was not till then that the results of that teaching were made manifest. Then the promise of the Spirit being fulfilled, those seeds of truth which had lain germinating in many hearts sprang to the light, and such mighty changes were wrought in the souls of men and in the relations of society, that the world looked on in bewilderment and admiration. These changes affected the whole sphere of life and duty, and among the virtues which received a mighty impulse was benevolence. Rendering a literal obedience to the Master's command, many of the early Christians actually sold their possessions and threw the price into a common fund, from which the wants of all were supplied. Nothing could teach more emphatically that the religion of Christ adopts and still further develops the practice of giving to God, which characterised the religion of the Jew, and that if Judaism and Christianity differ respecting that practice, the difference consists only in this, that the claims of Christ are greater and more strongly enforced than those of Moses, as the channels in which Christian charity may flow are broader and more numerous.

Wherever the Gospel was carried, the practice of contributing for its support and extension was introduced. We gather this from numerous allusions in the letters of Paul. Some churches were renowned for their proficiency in this "grace," for so the Apostle calls it. Of the churches of Macedonia in particular, he speaks in terms of warm commendation, as having both maintained a firm and joyful trust in God at a time of great affliction, and out of deep poverty ministered very liberally to the wants of the still more necessitous saints at Jerusalem. "To their power, I bear record," he says, "yea, and beyond their power they were willing of themselves; praying us with much intreaty that we would receive the gift, and take upon us the fellowship of the ministering to the saints." Writing to the Corinthians, Paul uses all the tact of which he was so consummate a master, in order to provoke them to a like generosity. Corinth was one of the wealthiest and most luxurious cities of Greece. The Macedonian churches were in deep poverty. But then as now, the poor out of their penury seem to have been giving far more than the rich out of their abundance. By alternate commendation and remonstrance, happy reference to liberal purposes once entertained, and mildly hinted rather than expressed reproof of their tardiness in executing them, the apostle seeks to stir them up to abound, as in other Christian graces, so in this also.

It is in the course of one of these epistles that the remarkable passage occurs, in which Paul propounds what may fairly be described as the apostolic method of Christian giving. "Now concerning the collection for the saints, as I have given order to the churches of Galatia, even so do ye. Upon the first day of the week let every one of you lay by him in store, as God hath prospered him, that there be no gatherings when I come." These words will in a future chapter receive our closer attention. At present we confine ourselves to a few general remarks on them. It is evident that the method which they describe had been devised by the apostle after careful consideration, that it was authoritatively prescribed, and that it was already in use among other churches. It was exceedingly simple, and well adapted on that very account to secure a sufficient revenue to meet all the outlay of the Church, and more particularly, in this instance, to provide for the poor saints at Jerusalem. Every one was to give. No definite proportion is mentioned as constituting a reasonable *minimum*, the reason probably being, that in the state and temper of the Church at that time, abounding as it did in the spirit of zeal and liberality, the mention of a *minimum* was wholly unnecessary. To enforce the duty of giving a tenth to the Lord was superfluous, when those addressed were already giving much more. And this seems to have been the case in most of the churches.

Thus we have reviewed both the precepts which are found in the Scriptures bearing upon this duty of giving, and the illustrious examples of men by whom these precepts were conscientiously obeyed. The conclusion to which the evidence we have had submitted to us seems to lead, may be summed up in a few words. We are taught to regard giving as essentially an act of worship, required both as a proof of the sincerity of our religion, and as an integral part of it. We are instructed that to acknowledge the proprietorship and sovereignty of God, and His great goodness to us, by devoting to His service a portion of the wealth which He Himself has given us, is, as much as the payment of debts due to our fellow-men, a duty binding on the Christian conscience. The amount claimed by God is in proportion to the amount with which He has entrusted us, but in no case do we find any less proportion than a tenth mentioned, while there are many instances given of much greater liberality. Those who practically recognise these obligations are blessed by God both with spiritual and with temporal blessings. Love to our fellow-men, such as exists wherever there is a sincere profession of Christianity, dictates the sacrifice of our own comforts, and even if need be, the limitation of our own supply of the necessaries of life, to secure the well-being of others. Giving, we are further taught, is to be at once intelligent and devout, prompt and cheerful, and in order that there may be a readiness to meet all pressing claims without trouble or confusion, the practice of storing the Lord's portion on the first day of the week is enjoined by the Apostle Paul on the early churches, and was very largely, if not universally, practised by them.

CHAPTER V.

THE CHURCH'S OBLIGATION TO GIVE.

Having set forth in the two previous chapters the teaching of Scripture with regard to the duty of giving, we propose to consider under what obligation that teaching lays the Church of these days. Our position is very different from that of the ancient Church. We do not now possess either the open vision or the miraculous word. We have now no prophets speaking with divine authority as moved by the Holy Ghost, no voices crying in the wilderness, and calling upon men in the name of God to cease to do evil and to learn to do well, no apostles unfolding with a power which drove conviction irresistibly to the heart, what they themselves had heard, had seen with their eyes, had looked upon, and their hands had handled,—that which was from the beginning, the Word of Life. The Church of Christ is now under the guidance of the written word and of the Spirit. If the Christian of modern times would know his duty, he must not wait for its announcement to him by an angel from heaven, or by a second Moses, or a second Paul. He must diligently consult the lively oracles of God, availing himself of all helps to understanding, such as those furnished by faithful expounders, and he must wait upon God in earnest prayer, and still praying, wait. Now as of old, faith is the first, the last, and the constant condition both of the recognition and acknowledgment of duty, and of that sense of obligation which compels performance. Do we indeed and in truth believe in God? Has faith in Him as the Rewarder of them that diligently seek Him a place in the inmost chamber of the heart? Do we accept the Scriptures as His word, and do we believe in the reality of a way even now open between earth and heaven, along which the prayers of men may pass to the throne of God, there to plead and to prevail? If there be such faith, the settlement of all questions of duty is easily and quickly effected. Where there is no such faith, the voice of Moses and the voice of Christ are uttered equally in vain.

What, then, is the light in which the Scripture testimony just adduced presents the duty of the Church in modern times? To those who believe that the Scriptures are given by inspiration of God, that they contain the wisdom of God, and that they are intended for the instruction and direction of the Church to the end of time, this inquiry will be of the first importance. In all that relates to the Church, the foolishness of God is wiser than men, and the weakness of God is stronger than men. It is to our loss and spiritual hurt that we disregard the commands or even the suggestions of the word, whether in matters of church order or of private duty. It is in vain that we substitute for divinely appointed plans and methods the most plausible and promising devices of our own. "To the law and to the testimony, if they speak not according to this word, it is because there is no light in them." It is quite true that the path of duty is not in all cases strictly defined. It is also true that many observances which were required of God's people in ancient times are no longer enforced.

The law, which was merely a shadow of good things to come, has ceased to be all that it once was, now that the substance has been revealed. Many of its requirements are obsolete in the letter, though they still survive in the spirit. But these considerations do not weaken the authority of Scripture or render its guidance doubtful. They only impose upon us the necessity of diligent search and discrimination, in order that we may distinguish clearly what the Spirit saith unto the Church, not of ancient Israel, but of modern Britain, not of the first century, but of the nineteenth.

The obligation to give is so generally acknowledged, that our attention will be chiefly directed to the further and more vexed question of the proportion which should be given. Many who have carefully inquired into this matter have come to the conclusion, that the rule of contributing one-tenth was prescribed by God from the earliest times, and that it was intended to remain perpetually in force. They admit that the law of Moses contains the first recorded formal declaration of the rule, but they argue that the incidental mention of the practice of it by Abraham and Jacob, proves that it was known and honoured from the first. In this respect they maintain that it holds a position analogous to that held by the institution of the Sabbath, which God ordained at the creation of the world, and even then made of perpetual and world-wide obligation, and which consequently does not cease to be binding on the consciences of men, because the ceremonial law, which recognised it and gave minute directions for the manner of its observance, has been abrogated. This view, however, does not altogether commend itself to us, our objection to it being, not that it is too stringent or that it exacts too much, but that it lacks evidence, and that it fixes, as of divine and permanent appointment, a limit within which the liberality of a more ardent and zealous Christianity has never been confined. The brief statements respecting the practice of Abraham and Jacob, though they may justify us in inferring the existence of a custom of systematic giving, prior to their times, are scarcely such as to warrant the conclusion that a positive law determining the proportion had already been promulgated. And even if the existence of such a law could be established, we are not disposed to admit that it would occupy the same ground as that law of the Sabbath, the perpetual obligation of which Christians acknowledge. It would rather have a place in the same category with those definite and formal regulations for the keeping of the Sabbath by Israel, the need for which does not exist under the Christian dispensation.

Passing to the consideration of the law of giving laid down by Moses, we fail to discover any signs of universality and perpetuity in its apportionment of one-tenth of the increase. We must remember that the Children of Israel were as children under a tutor, and that partly from their own ignorance and spiritual obtuseness, and partly from the dimness which still hung over the spiritual and the heavenly, the Sun of Righteousness not yet having risen in splendour, they were unable to appreciate or to use such glorious liberty as that with which Christ makes his people free, and needed a strict and almost palpable demarcation of duty. The recognition of the need of the strictly defined is evident in the Mosaic economy from beginning to end, just as in the New Testament we have a reiterated recognition of the sufficiency of Christian grace without positive law, as superseding law by more than fulfilling it.

Our conclusion then is, that in determining how much

to give, we are to be guided not so much by the letter of the law as by its spirit; not so much by the positive institutions of Moses, as by the principles inculcated and the motives supplied by Christ. Whether these lead to the adoption of a lower or a higher standard of liberality we must now consider. The question being one of comparison between the Jewish and the Christian dispensations, we may profitably refer to that elaborate exposition of the relations subsisting between them which is found in the Epistle to the Hebrews. There the superiority of the new to the old is indicated and studiously set forth. Its Mediator is shown to be the Mediator of a better covenant; it is established on better promises, it furnishes a better sacrifice, it provides better things, it inspires with a better hope. In what direction do these changes tend but to the raising up of a better seed to Abraham,—spiritual children who shall be kings and priests to God, devoted to His service, devising liberal things for the extension of His Kingdom, and in their gifts of substance to His cause passing far beyond the minimum of liberality required of the newly emancipated and still half-idolatrous Israel? The progress from the old to the new is one of growing spirituality, the gradual depreciation of mere earthly good, and the attachment of a correspondingly increasing value to that which is heavenly and real. In Christ himself we find this progress culminating. It was the prospect of obtaining one narrow country, flowing with milk and honey, that drew the Children of Israel from Egypt. Christ beheld unmoved all the kingdoms of the world and the glory of them spread out before Him, and the offer of them all was resolutely and unhesitatingly set aside. The same spirit of indifference to the world in the presence of the surpassing splendour of the heavenly Kingdom dwelt in the apostles and especially in Paul. He could say, "What things were gain to me those I counted loss for Christ. Yea, doubtless, and I count all things but loss for the excellency of the knowledge of Christ Jesus my Lord." Now it is written with the pen of inspiration, that if any man have not the spirit of Christ, he is none of His. It is the utterance of this spirit therefore that we must seek, when we desire to know how much is due to the cause of God and of humanity. That spirit of wisdom which so justly estimated the relative value of things, beginning with the declaration that the life is more than meat and the body than raiment, and passing on to assign a greater value to the salvation of a soul than to the acquisition of a world, is alone competent satisfactorily to determine the question, "How much owest thou unto my Lord?"

Of old the believers sold their possessions and laid the price at the apostles' feet. We are not required to act in the same manner, but just in proportion as our Christianity is sincere and earnest we shall be found acting in the same spirit. Money will be lightly esteemed in comparison with the Kingdom of God, and in our disposal of it a regard to the interests of the Kingdom will have the greatest weight. This spirit of heavenly wisdom, the spirit of Christ, may lead to various action, according to the circumstances and idiosyncrasies of each. One may be led like the poor widow to cast in all his living into the treasury. Another, like John Wesley, may be led to reduce his personal expenditure to what is required for the barest necessaries of life, and to disburse his entire remaining income in deeds of charity and in the furtherance of religion. A third may be guided to employ his capital in business, and to give a proportion of his annual profits to the direct advancement of truth and righteousness. But we venture to express the belief, that in no case where there is an intelligent and sincere profession of that Christianity which is so greatly in advance of Judaism, will there be a falling short of the standard of liberality which even Judaism prescribed. Wherever the love of Christ exercises a constraining power, and is accompanied by an actual knowledge of the grace that was in Him, how that "for our sakes He became poor, that we through His poverty might be rich," there will certainly be found a readiness to will, and a performance also out of that which we have. It is not asserted that there can be no Christianity without the manifestation of a greater than Jewish liberality. There are weak Christians, and Christians wanting in an intelligent apprehension of the nature and obligations of their faith, as there are also Christians living in the neglect of known privileges and the repudiation of known responsibility. We do not refuse the title 'Christian' because of every inconsistency. But surely no one will dispute the statement, that if the Jew was rightly called on to devote a tenth or a fifth of the increase of his substance year by year to God, the Christian cannot with due regard to his loftier spiritual privileges, larger sphere of influence, and more powerfully constraining motives, offer less. The law is not made for the righteous man but for the lawless and disobedient. The Christian who has strong faith in his Christianity and who lavishes his treasure in advancing its ends, not casting one regretful look on what he is sacrificing for Christ, is hampered by no positive regulations. He obeys the law of love, and he finds a blessedness in his free obedience which conformity to a positive regulation could never confer. But only those who have attained to this truly Christian liberality have ceased to have to do altogether with the law of the tenth. For all others it still stands, not indeed as a measure of what is required of them, but as a reproach to them that they have not passed beyond, perhaps have not even reached, what was fixed as the lowest proportion in a time of pupilage and of comparative darkness. A tenth at least, in order that the men of a past generation may not rise up to condemn us; as much more as we can or will in order that we may illustrate the freer and more generous, the more magnanimous and more loving genius of Christianity— such is practically the decision of Scripture. To men of wealth, whose income far exceeds their expenditure, be it framed on ever so liberal or ever so lavish a scale, there is a loud call to give more than a tenth. Of what avail is it to heap up a colossal fortune, which must soon be left to others, and which in the course of a generation or two may be inherited by a fool, who will dissipate it in wickedness and folly, at which he who accumulated it, could he have foreseen the future, would have stood aghast. To lay out wisely in works tending to the good of men and the glory of God, not a tenth or even a fifth, but a third or a half of the annual income, would be as prudent in many an affluent man as it would be consistent with a sincere, intelligent, and devout profession of Christianity.

To plead the abrogation of the Jewish law of tithe as an excuse for not devoting even a tenth to God, is practically to express a want of confidence in the future of the Church of Christ, to repudiate the infinite obligation under which the Saviour has placed the souls which He has redeemed, and to ignore what Christ has taught, both in regard to the first and great commandment of the law—" Thou shalt love the Lord thy God with all thy heart and soul and mind," and in regard to that second which is like to it—"Thou shalt love thy neighbour as thyself." We are well aware that to utter these truths is to take up a position which many are not prepared to occupy. But is it not evident from a comparison of the brilliant success of Christianity in the first age, with its slower progress in recent times, that some fatal inconsistency is weakening its strength in the way and unfitting it for aggressive action ? And to what may we so reasonably attribute this weakness as to the almost universal failure of the Church to look fairly and steadily at its obligations and to set itself to their discharge ; to realise the height and greatness of its calling, and to aim with singleness of purpose at its fulfilment ? If every Christian were by personal effort, or by gifts of his substance for the support of the minister or the missionary, to be instrumental in the conversion of only one soul every year, in fifteen years a church having a membership equal to that of the United Presbyterian Church would evangelize the world, and secure the whole of its population of twelve hundred millions for Christ. If so great an aggregate of work could be accomplished by the accumulating power of so small an amount of individual effort, how do the insignificant results after the lapse of eighteen centuries rise up in judgment against the Church and condemn it ! With a mission so great, with a gospel so powerful, with Christ at its head, and his Spirit as its Teacher and Comforter, why has not the Church accomplished more ? The reasons are suggested by that promise of Christ—" According to your faith be it unto you," and that sad question which He proposed —" When the Son of Man cometh shall He find faith on the earth ?" It is mainly because Christians have too much loved the world, and have timidly shrunk from casting their care upon the Lord, that they have accomplished so little. The cowardice and distrust which betrayed Ananias and Sapphira into their awful sin, have enervated many. They have clung tenaciously to the seen and temporal, and have not gone forth leaning with the arm of faith on the divine promises, seeking the better country, even the heavenly. There has been too often side by side with the willingness to trust all to Christ for the salvation of the soul in the world to come, a resolute exclusion of Him from authority and control in things pertaining to the present. In such a state of the Church, it is to be expected that a reiteration of the old statements of the claims of Christ will meet with the same reception which these statements themselves met when first propounded. They will be found still as of old hard sayings, and many will be unable to bear them. But if there be a falling off of many in Israel as the result of declaring any truth, it can only be the precursor of the rising of many. The claims of Christ are based on a broad and deep foundation of truth and equity. It is as impossible to plead them too plainly or too urgently, as it is to respond to them too liberally. If the conduct of a poor widow giving her all was approved, we need not fear that any gifts of ours will provoke his censure as being unwarrantably great. What the Church needs is more heroism—a mind to grasp the glorious far-off future, a heart to devise liberal things to bring it about, hands that both labour and give in order to secure it, and through all, a firm faith that takes Christ at His word, looks to Him for its reward, and endures as seeing Him.

There are three sentences of Christ's, bearing on this duty, which are worthy of special consideration by Christian Britain. One is the injunction—" Freely ye have received, freely give." Obligation is here made commensurate with privilege, and if this be the rule of the Kingdom, how great must the obligation be which rests upon the Church in this country. When we consider all that has been bestowed upon our island, the freedom which we enjoy, the stability of our institutions, the long and undisturbed peace which has reigned within our borders, the diffusion of knowledge among our population, our immense natural resources, our amazing manufacturing industries, our gigantic trade and commerce, our political power, our naval supremacy, our possession of an empire on which the sun never sets, and above all our free and unrestricted access to the word of God, both as issued from the press and as declared from the pulpit, we are forced to confess that "God has not dealt so with any nation." Britain has, indeed, in respect to privilege, been exalted to heaven. For what purposes have this pre-eminence been assigned to her? For what purposes has she been entrusted with these unparalleled opportunities? Has it been merely that she may be clothed in fine linen and purple and scarlet, and decked with gold and precious stones and pearls, that she may glorify herself, and live deliciously, and say in her heart, "I sit as queen;" that the merchants of the earth may wax rich through the multitude of her delicacies, and that her merchants may be the great men of the earth? Or has it not rather been that she may be as a city set on an hill, and that from her, lines may go forth to all the earth, and a word to the end of the world? Has it not been that she may say among the heathen that the Lord reigneth, and utter in the ear of the nations the invocation, "Give unto the Lord, O ye kindreds of the people, give unto the Lord glory and strength, give unto the Lord the glory due unto His name?" Alas, how often are our wise men found glorying in their wisdom, and our mighty men glorying in their might, and our rich men glorying in their riches! When shall the time come when it will be the glory of the inhabitants of our land that the nation understands and knows God, that He is the Lord who exercises loving-kindness, judgment, and righteousness in the earth, and delights in these things? When shall British power be chiefly exerted to secure for dwellers in distant lands the right of worshipping God, each one under his own vine and fig-tree, none daring to make afraid? When shall the broad streams of British commerce, instead of carrying to less enlightened nations the alcohol and the opium that curse with a deadly curse the loveliest lands and the noblest races, bear upon them in going and returning the goodly merchandise of the Kingdom? When shall British gold, instead of remaining locked up in the coffers into which it has flowed from the four quarters of the globe, or being dissipated in selfish and hurtful luxuriousness, be employed in sending the Gospel, with all its civilising influences, to those millions of toiling and suffering men and women, by the sweat of whose brows, often at the expense of whose tears and blood, it has been acquired?

But we need not go abroad to be reminded of the necessity of giving freely; in our own cities, at our own doors, we have "the masses." Side by side with the accumulation of wealth and the advance in refinement and luxury among the religious, there is progressing a terrible deterioration among those who threaten to become the majority in our land. The unequal distribution of labour devolving excessive burdens on many, the evil influence of crowding in our cities, of badly-arranged houses, and of the violation of sanitary principles, the disastrous results of imperfect education, and of the existence of a vast number of public-houses and other places of temptation to intemperance and crime, with other more obscure causes, are constantly operating to swell the number of those who are outside of all our religious denominations, and to sink them deeper and yet deeper in their apparently hopeless degradation. We boast of the wealth and splendour of London and Glasgow and Liverpool. But how little reason is there for such boasting? Does not the cry of those multitudes of human souls who are being offered as a sacrifice on the altar of Moloch enter into the ears of the God of Sabaoth, and will He not hear their cry? Every unit in that surging crowd is an individual soul with thoughts, feelings, hopes, fears, and purposes, with a heaven to gain and a hell to flee from, with a God on high, whom in all its degradation and shame it is still permitted to address as Father. The shoeless, ragged, hungry child is the object of that Heavenly Father's regard equally with the luxuriously attired and daintily-fed *millionaire*. God thinks upon the one as upon the other, and He will mete out impartial justice to both. "The rich and the poor meet together, the Lord is the maker of them all." It is in vain that the opulent seek to free themselves from responsibility in connection with this abounding ignorance and degradation. The causes which have been at work to accumulate enormous wealth in the hands of the few, have indirectly contributed in large measure to the evils existing in the condition of the many. No man has a right to grow rich by means which even indirectly impoverish or degrade his fellow-men. When such impoverishment or degradation is found to attend his progress, considerations of mere justice oblige him to apply the first portions of the wealth he has acquired in compensating the general society for the loss occasioned to it. When Christianity takes full possession of the minds and hearts of its professors, men of wealth will be found giving more attention to the sources of their wealth and the history of its accumulation, that they may redress wrongs unwittingly inflicted in the course of its acquisition, and that they may counteract or mitigate, if they cannot prevent, the evils indirectly entailed by the industries from which it has been derived.

The second of the suggestive passages referred to occurs in the account of the last entry into Jerusalem. The disciples were instructed to bring for the Master's use an ass and its foal which they would find in a certain place, and if any one objected they were to reply, "The Lord hath need of them," and he would send them straightway. The owner of the animals was doubtless one who recognised the claims of the Lord, and so he no sooner learned that the request came from Jesus than he was ready cheerfully to comply. With regard to our silver and our gold, the words may be used with equal truth, "The Lord hath need of them." There are, it is true, some who object to such statements. "God has no need either of man's work or of his money," they reply; "what He wills, He accomplishes by His own mighty power. It approaches the blasphemous to speak of Him, whose are all things, as having need of the paltry gifts of His creatures." In one sense these are true utterance, but in another they are misleading. God has no absolute need of anything. But it has pleased Him to make human wills and human hearts and hands instrumental in the accomplishment of His great purposes, and in this sense it is true even of the Lord, that He has need. Jesus was poor and needy when He passed through the world, all things in which had been made by Him. He stood in need of the ministration of the devoted women who followed Him. He stood in need of, and gratefully accepted offices of love from those who believed in Him. "The poor ye have always with you, but Me ye have not always," He said to one who objected to a tribute of this kind which had just been rendered. It was not indeed to receive such tributes that He came to our world. "The Son of Man came not to be ministered unto but to minister." But His requirement and acceptance of the ministrations of men, whether to Himself personally, as when He was on the earth, or to the least of His brethren, form part of the fulfilment of His ministry.

If the Lord then has need, who among his followers will say aught except in the way of cheerfully acceding to His requests. And has He not need of the silver and gold of His people? Hundreds of churches need to be built, the ministry needs to be supported, missionaries need to be equipped and sent forth, neglected children need to be educated in the Sunday School, the Bible needs to be circulated throughout the world, the poor need to be encouraged and strengthened, hospitals for the destitute, sick and dying, and asylums for the orphans and the fatherless, need to be provided and maintained, and money is needed for all these beneficent works. Christ himself asks it from us. When money is required for other purposes, it is very readily forthcoming. We can invest one hundred and seventeen millions in the liquor traffic, and we can erect public-houses in such numbers that in our large cities there is one to every thirty or thirty-five families. We can expend one hundred and forty millions in one year on intoxicating drinks, the larger proportion of this expendiure being by common consent the purchase money of disease, poverty and crime. We can dissipate twenty millions annually on the questionable luxury of tobacco. We can lavish one hundred millions in two years on a war waged to protect the real or imaginary interests of the empire, and the nation would be prepared to expend much more, if necessary, to avenge an insult to its flag. When the messengers of Christ, then, approach us, and ask our co-operation in a work the most benignant, the farthest reaching, the most glorious, and the most certain of ultimate success, and when pointing to the silver and gold passing through our hands or stored in our coffers, they say to us in His name "the Lord hath need of them," is there not an overwhelming obligation to consider intelligently, devoutly, and carefully the claims thus advanced, and to act in accordance with the conclusion at which the Christian conscience and the Christian heart may arrive?

In connection with this aspect of the question, the parable of the talents is brought vividly before us, and the memorable words, "Occupy till I come," take a place by the side of those already mentioned. The stewardship of the Christian is one of time, energy, and influence, but it also extends to money. And he would be the most faithful and the most approved steward with respect to his use of this talent, who, setting aside all ideas of personal indulgence and ease, should seek only so to use his money as to make it secure in the largest measure those results which are precious in the sight of Christ. Yet how seldom does the Christian in the course of his calculations with respect either to the acquisition or the expenditure of wealth, take the interests of Christ's Kingdom into the question as properly belonging to it. It is to be feared that many transactions on both sides of the account are such as will not bear inspection by the Master's eye. Even our givings to the cause of religion and benevolence are often more than neutralised by our indirect contributions on the other hand to the cause of the Adversary. Too many while professedly building up are indirectly pulling down, and the work of demolition too often proceeds more steadily and effectually than that of restoration. How lamentably is this the case in our relations with ignorant and barbarous peoples! We go to them carrying the Bible in the one hand to bless, and in the other the fiery spirit or the deadly opium to curse and destroy. Alas! all the good effected by the one is scarcely an equivalent for the evil, destined to deepen and spread, throughout many generations, wrought by the other.

In getting or in giving, the Christian is to remember his stewardship, the true function of which is neither the accumulation nor the disbursement of wealth, but the use of it in such ways and with such diligence as to bring down and diffuse blessing, and to help on the time when, in the language of prophecy, Christ "shall see of the travail of his soul and be satisfied." The charge "to occupy until He come," addresses itself with great urgency to men of wealth. To them this talent of money has been specially entrusted. The accumulation of the power belonging to money is in their hands and subject to their control. A day is coming when an account must be rendered, and then it will be seen how far the golden stream, in influx and reflux under their direction, carried upon its bosom peace and righteousness and joy, and aided in the diffusion of these blessings among men; or how far it was a source of corruption, carrying in its course an atmosphere of spiritual degradation and death. Happy those servants who at the coming of their Lord shall be able to give in an account of money, so acquired and so expended as to advance the ends dear to His heart!

To them the thrilling words of approval and acceptance will be addressed, "Well done, good and faithful servant, enter thou into the joy of thy Lord! Thou hast been faithful over a few things, I will make thee ruler over many things!" On the other hand, how sad and humiliating will then be the issue of a thousand laborious and so-called successful careers, how startling the collapse of a thousand reputations which in their day filled the world, when the rich who neither feared God nor regarded man, shall be addressed as wicked and slothful servants, and hear the doom of their unfaithfulness pronounced. On earth they were not unwarned. The spirit of God had thus addressed them, "Go to now, ye rich men, weep and howl for your miseries that shall come upon you. Your gold and silver is cankered, and the rust of them shall be a witness against you, and shall eat your flesh as it were fire. Ye have heaped treasure together for the last days." But they despised the admonition, and now the distress and anguish have come upon them, and all the gentle expostulations, the earnest entreaties, the words of warning and reproof which, had they been entertained, might have led to repentance, are converted into stings which pierce them with bitter regrets, as they view in retrospect life wasted, trust misplaced, and gracious opportunities of obtaining a place and a name in the Kingdom neglected and now lost for ever.

CHAPTER VI.

EXISTING METHODS AND THEIR RESULTS.

IN the previous chapter we have been considering chiefly the obligation resting on the Church to give liberally to the service of God. In the present chapter we propose to inquire how far this obligation is generally recognised, in what manner it is met, and to what extent it is discharged. We shall begin with the third of these interesting inquiries, and as the readiest way to a definite conclusion we shall compare the amounts dedicated by the nation at large to religious purposes, with the amounts expended in various ways to secure real or supposed personal advantages. It is very difficult to ascertain the exact amount contributed for the support of Churches, and the carrying on of the operations of missionary and benevolent societies, but taking published statistics as the basis of our calculation we make a liberal allowance when we set down the total as being rather less than twenty millions. The total income of the country has been estimated at £1,000,000,000. It would thus appear that the proportion in which wealthy England dedicates her wealth to God, so far from exceeding the tenth required of ancient Israel, only amounts to one-fiftieth. If we confine our attention to giving for church purposes, the result is equally humiliating. Let us examine the statistics of the United Presbyterian Church, which is certainly not behind any of the Christian denominations in liberality. In 1874 that Church numbered 187,761 communicants, representing, let us say, a total membership, including children, of not less than 500,000. During the same year the income of the

Church from all sources amounted to about £365,000. This gives fourteen shillings as the rate of contribution per individual. Let us compare this with the amount per head which the country spends in various other ways. The cost of the tobacco consumed in the United Kingdom during 1874 amounted to £20,000,000, or rather more than thirteen shillings per head of the population. So that supposing the liberality of the United Presbyterian Church in giving for church support reached by all other denominations we have still the fact before us that we give, for the building of churches and the support of the gospel ministry, an amount which is hardly in excess of our expenditure on a doubtful, and in very many cases a confessedly hurtful, luxury. During 1874 the national drink bill amounted to £140,000,000. Contrast with this the sum total of £20,000,000, contributed to the cause of religion and benevolence! Mr Hoyle of Manchester, an able statistician, reckons the aggregate annual waste in useless but fashionable display at £120,000,000. A writer in *Fraser's Magazine* (October 1872), who furnishes the elaborate calculations on which his results are based, arrives at the conclusion that £370,000,000 of our total annual income are spent on luxuries by 450,000 families, or about 2,000,000 of the population. These figures are sufficiently suggestive. God blesses us with an agriculture, with manufactures, with trade and commerce, which bring in a thousand millions annually. Of that we spend about four hundred millions in all to provide for factitious wants, including one hundred and forty millions for strong drink and twenty millions for tobacco. And then having clothed ourselves with the finest vestments, having eaten and drunken and made merry, we lay twenty millions upon the altar of God for the maintenance of that religion, and those charities, to which we yet dare to refer as the source and safeguard of our national prosperity; and out of the thousand millions which He entrusts to us, and which He bids us occupy till He come, we devote one million to the work of evangelising the world. From Africa, Asia and America, and from the islands of the sea, the labour and the natural wealth of a hundred races flow to our shores, enriching our people and making our merchants princes. These races are sitting in darkness and in the shadow of death. Their cry is, Come over and help us. Christ pleads in their behalf. Our own material interests even might lead us to listen to their appeal. The vastness of the expectant multitude demands a liberal response. We look over our thousand millions, and after spending one hundred and forty on intoxicating drinks we set aside for the conversion of the heathen, one!

Such are the results of existing methods. Are they satisfactory? No Christian will for a moment hesitate as to the answer. If this be the manner in which, as a nation, we discharge the duties of our stewardship, may we not expect the Lord to come speedily and to say to us, "Give an account of your stewardship, for ye may no longer be stewards." The lavish expenditure of money on luxury and in dissipation, the eager and unscrupulous haste to be rich in order to be able so to spend, the narrowness of mind and closeness of hand manifested when the claims of the Kingdom are urged, are features of the time full of evil omen; and if increasing wealth continue to be accompanied by increasing waste, and the multiplication of opportunities by a more shameful misimprovement of them, nothing will save our country from the curse which lighted on Capernaum and Bethsaida.

We must now turn from the contemplation of these

depressing statistics, and direct our attention to such views, dispositions, and habits of the Christian people, as are related to the subject of giving. The causes of our failure, as a nation, to give in adequate measure to the service of God, lie deep in the minds and hearts of individuals, and we must seek out the root of the evil there, if we would understand it and be able to suggest a remedy. We dismiss, then, those enormous amounts with which we have been dealing, and confine our attention to the receipts and disbursements of the individual. Just as the mightiest rivers are fed by streamlets, and these streamlets by rills, which again draw their supplies from the drops of rain and dew, so that he who would fully understand the history and character of the mighty flood rolling on in grandeur and might to the sea, must examine it at its source, and take account of the streamlets and rills which combine to form it; so the figures which embody the aggregate results of Christian giving do not of themselves furnish us with a satisfactory account of its origin or its amount. We must look at the subject from the standpoint of the individual giver, and seek to understand his views, motives, purposes, and fulfilment. Thus only we shall be able to indicate what is faulty or weak, and to suggest how theory may be rectified and consistency in practice secured.

Such an investigation reveals the existence of three prevalent hindrances to the replenishment of the Lord's treasury, Selfishness, Inconsiderateness, and Want of System in giving. With the first of these it is not our business to deal at any great length in a work of this nature. It is an evil which lies embedded in the human heart, and against which the gospel needs to exert its utmost power. The question, "Am I my

F

brother's keeper?" is often prompted by it. It diligently concentrates attention on its own things, and refuses to obey the apostolic precept, "to look every man also on the things of others." In its extreme form it has a clearly marked policy, and one to which it tenaciously adheres, namely, to get all that it can and to give as little as it dare. And there are those to whom it would not be just to ascribe selfishness in this its lowest type, who yet are governed by the thought that what is given to the Church, or to charity, is in a manner lost, and that what can be held back from these is in a manner gained. An exorbitant estimate has been formed by them of the importance of their own comfort, convenience, or satisfaction, and they fail to sympathise with the deepest sorrows and the most pressing wants of others. Even the sacred claims of justice, and the quick, authoritative promptings of honourable dealing, are disregarded where this spirit of absorbing and exclusive devotion to self reigns. Those of whom it takes possession easily reconcile themselves to the meanness of appropriating all that is placed within their reach, whether of temporal or of spiritual good, and rendering no adequate acknowledgment, either to God the Supreme Bestower, or to those who minister His holy things, and regarding whom He has appointed that they shall live of the Gospel.

Against this evil it is vain to use arguments or to adduce statistics. Selfishness can only be overcome by the grace of God acting on the heart through the Gospel itself. The sinner who has been under deep conviction of sin, and who is now freed from the terrors of the law by faith in Christ, is invariably ready to respond to appeals on behalf of that Gospel which he has found so precious, of that Saviour who died for him, and of those still unbelieving and impenitent souls, the sadness of whose condition his own recent experience enables him vividly to realise. It is this ardour of the first love which explains the munificence of the early Church, just after its formation. Those people of Jerusalem had just been forgiven much,—their complicity in the death of Christ,—and they loved much. No power in the universe can so melt a hard heart and disarm a selfish spirit as the Gospel, which holds forth a crucified Saviour, can. Here we perceive the bearing of all faithful preaching of the Gospel on the increase of liberality in the Church. A forcible representation of gospel truth, such as awakens the soul to the terrible realities of sin, and the glorious all-sufficiency of the Saviour, is certain to evoke a spirit of self-denial and of consecration in believing hearts, and to lead to the enlistment of many as earnest labourers for Christ.

Inconsiderateness is, in many instances, perhaps we should say in very many, to be charged with the paucity and the paltriness of Christian offerings. The donors are neither constitutionally nor habitually selfish, but in forming their habits of giving they have been governed by the example of others, or by general usage, rather than by regard to the voice of conscience or the promptings of a grateful heart; and having once fixed upon certain absolute amounts, they have continued to give these year after year under every variety of fortune, and in many cases notwithstanding an enormous increase in ability. There are multitudes who never ask themselves the question, How much do I owe to Christ? or, How much ought I to give for the advancement of truth and righteousness? but with whom the determining consideration is the amount expected by collectors or applicants, or the amount given by neighbours, or the amount which it may be convenient just at the time to spare. Some may feel disposed to attach but light blame to the remissness which is due to this want of independent thought, nevertheless it justly incurs the Saviour's reproof and admonition, "Be watchful and strengthen the things which remain, which are ready to die : for I have not found thy works perfect before God." Civil governments and military rulers inflict heavy penalties for such neglect or inconsiderateness as lead to loss of life, or other serious consequences; and he is not held guiltless in the court of heaven who sleeps at his post, or allows himself to be imposed upon by counterfeit signs, when interests of such moment as the stability and extension of the Kingdom are at stake. Besides, although this inconsiderateness is not in itself selfishness, it springs from it. Let it be a question of acquiring property instead of a question of parting with it, and at once the faculties are in active exercise to ascertain the exact amount which may be justly claimed. No rough-and-ready calculations, no tender of a round sum, which may or may not be far below the amount justly obtainable, are admissible in this case. An inconsiderateness which only shows itself in the neglect to discover the amount of our indebtedness, and in the proffering of a sum which falls far short of that amount, has an appearance of being something more reprehensible than the comparatively innocent absence of mind which we might at first sight take it to be.

But besides selfishness and want of thought, there is a third cause which contributes very largely to the unsatisfactoriness of the sum-total of our national offerings, namely, the unsystematic character of most giving. The great majority give the bulk of what they do give, fitfully. Fixed small contributions to special objects may be given at stated times, but the larger gifts are presented at irregular periods; the only rule being that one such extraordinary act of liberality shall not follow too closely upon the heel of another. Mr A., a wealthy man, is called upon by Mr X., and is solicited for a subscription towards the building of a new church in the neighbourhood. The cause is good, and Mr A. in his heart approves of it, but only yesterday he handed a cheque for £10 to Mr Y., towards the salary of the town missionary, and so he puts on a resolute air, and says that " He really must decline. The calls are so numerous that he finds it impossible to respond to them all." The cheque for £10 signed within the last twenty-four hours is before him, and, " to give again at so brief an interval —that sort of thing would never do. It would lead to bankruptcy." But Mr A. does not bear in mind that for some three or four months he has not parted with an equal sum for any religious or charitable purposes whatsoever, and that during that period his stated contributions to all Christian objects have made up an amount so small that he would be ashamed to have it thought of, or even himself to think of it, as the ordinary measure of his liberality. The truth is, that those who give in this unsystematic and spasmodic fashion seldom know how little they do give. The constantly recurring small contributions for church purposes, and the occasional larger donations to the church and for charity, make a deeper and more lasting impression upon the mind than the numerous little disbursements for personal gratification, and the occasional larger outlays for unnecessary and often foolish display. And thus those who keep no account of their givings, and who consequently have no opportunity for comparing the sum-total with other items of expenditure, are often surprised, when, on being induced to look into the matter, the true state of the beneficence account is revealed. That, in very many, inadequate giving is due to this want of system and not to active selfishness, is evident from the readiness and cheerfulness with which a reform is introduced when consideration has convinced them that it is needed.

Our common modes of raising money for church purposes take their character from the views, dispositions, and habits of the members of the Church, and when we have considered to how large an extent selfishness usurps the throne of the heart to the exclusion of the nobler spirit of the Gospel, and how inconsiderateness and unmethodical habits of giving are fostered by it, we are not surprised to find that the arrangements made for the raising of a church revenue are extremely faulty and inefficient. As the support of the Church and the Ministry constitutes the most important of all the objects to which God's portion is devoted, these arrangements require our more careful examination. Confining ourselves to those which are most extensively adopted, we have ; 1°, Seat-rents ; 2°, Ordinary church-door Collections ; 3°, Special Collections ; 4°, Ordinary weekly or monthly Subscriptions. And when some extraordinary demand for money arises, as in the building of a new church, or the renovation of an old one, the erection of a manse, the liquidation of debt, or the removal of a balance from the wrong side of a treasurer's account, other means are resorted to, among which may be noted, 1°, solicitation of aid from persons of known ability and willinghood, members of other congregations ; 2°, Bazaars ; 3°, Lectures, Amateur Concerts, Penny Readings, and Tea Meetings.

The exaction of Seat-rents is so old and universal a custom, that those who would interfere with it must expect to meet with much well-meaning opposition, and should be prepared with a very strong case. It is not difficult, however, to show that it is not the best means of supply, and that it does not even operate equitably and efficiently. In the first place, it is based on the ecclesiastical fiction that payment is rendered as an equivalent for the convenience and comfort of the accommodation provided. Every one knows that the money is applied mainly to the payment of the minister's stipend. There may not in some cases be much in a name, and many fictions of the legal and other sorts are innocent enough. But in this case a real evil often ensues. The renter of the pew having paid the sum fixed, has a consciousness of having fully met his obligations, and in this comfortable assurance, he occupies his place as a hearer of the Gospel Sabbath after Sabbath. He has met all demands. He is entitled to his pew, and he is not unfrequently jealous of his rights of proprietorship for the time being. The expenses of the Church may be heavy, and the membership may be small. The majority of the congregation may be poor, and there may thus be the need of greater liberality in the case of those well-to-do. But none of these things are brought home to him. He pays what he owes, and if things are not going on well, the fault must be elsewhere, as it does not lie with him. The result is that when the income of the Church is derived exclusively or even mainly from seat-rents, it often falls miserably short of the requirements. "We have sittings in the Church. We have paid the seat-rents." How often are people deluded by the ecclesiastical fiction into the belief that if they are able to say this, they have discharged their duty to the Church and to its Head as far as maintenance is concerned. The inequality of the system is also a serious objection to it. It makes little allowance for the widely differing circumstances of the worshippers in regard to worldly wealth. It is true that in many Churches there are pews at high rates and pews at low rates, pews for the rich and pews for the poor, but not to speak of the invidiousness of the distinction thus conspicuously drawn, the difference of the amounts asked seldom bears a reasonable proportion to the difference in the ability to pay. And thus it may happen that the man of large means, who has no family, and rents but one sitting, may be required to pay in this form very much less than his poor neighbour, who, for the accommodation of his wife and children, must rent a whole pew. Besides these objections, there is another, namely, that a seat-rent is a payment, and not a gift or offering. An "account" of what is due is made out, and the exact amount charged, and neither more nor less is looked for. The whole wears the aspect of an ordinary business transaction, rather than that of an act of worship, or of self-denial from regard to the claims of Christ and of his Church.

The inequality and insufficiency of the Seat-rent system are so apparent, that there are very few cases in which it is relied upon as the sole source of congregational income, other means being adopted to supplement it, and in particular, the Ordinary Collection at the church door. The custom of contributing in this form is not open to objection on the score of inequality or indirectness, and it can plead the highest and most ancient authority, for the Jews on entering the temple to take part in its service, were instructed to cast their gifts into the treasury. It admits also of the association of appropriate thoughts and feelings, and of prayer, with the act of presentation. Indeed, it is this mode of giving for church purposes which answers most fully to the ideal of a simple, equable, elastic, and sufficient method, and one in accordance with the nature of the ends sought. If it has not superseded all others, it is not because of its not excelling them in 'the estimation of most thoughtful Christian men, but because the Church has not had sufficient faith in it, and has not brought intelligence and loyalty to Christ sufficiently to bear in the mode of using it. As long as the church-door collection is only one of many sources of church income, and the amount contributed is only one of many amounts contributed for the same purpose, the people will be ruled in determining what they shall give, by custom or the example of others, or momentary inclination or convenience, rather than by the magnitude of the claims which have to be met. The weekly collection may be made, as we shall speedily endeavour to show, an unexceptionable means of supplying the treasury of the Church, and one in itself amply sufficient. But as it exists at present in many Churches, the "eleemosynary heap of bawbees" is not an encouraging sight to one who would fain retain such faith in the sincerity, intelligence, and heroism of the Christian Church, as would be implied in the act of casting the burden of all provision for its necessities upon the free-will offerings of the people.

Next on our list is the Special Collection. Every one is familiar with the "modus operandi" which among some religious communities, notably some south of the Tweed, has been brought to a high state of perfection. The services of a popular preacher are secured, placards are posted, announcing the sermons, handbills are distributed among members of other churches, the choir spends much time and labour in preliminary exercises, and in order that there may be absolute security against failure, it is in some places the practice to arrange beforehand the staff of collectors, with each of whom an understanding, tacit or expressed, exists as to the particular coin of the realm which he shall deposit in the plate as an example and encouragement to others. All the arrangements, those for the preaching of the Gospel included, are planned with regard to the one main object for the time being, the obtaining of the largest possible amount of money. Great and serious mischief often arises from these spasmodic efforts, and especially from the concentration of interest on the pecuniary result. After such services the one question is, How much was the collection? The proper ends of the preaching of the Gospel and the worship of God are in danger of being lost sight of, in the spiritual mammon-worship of the hour. The result depends much more on the eloquence and tact of the preacher and on the care bestowed on the arrangements, than on the goodness of the cause. Some preachers have even acquired a peculiar reputation for power in the pulpit of the kind that commands the pockets of the hearers, and such are greatly sought after on these occasions. But abnormal excitement is invariably followed by depression, and sometimes great collections are as ruinous to the finances of a Church as great victories have been to many mighty armies. The people depend upon them, and the springs of ordinary and habitual liberality are allowed to dry up. By-and-bye the enthusiasm of the periodical effort begins to flag. Stronger and stronger stimulants in larger measure become necessary to rouse to the former pitch of excitement. Nice scruples are disregarded in view of the imagined necessity of getting money by some means; scandals arise, and too often the result is the demoralisation and disintegration of Churches which, if they had been content to draw their support from the quiet and sustained liberality of their own members, might have had a history of steadily increasing prosperity and usefulness.

Of weekly or monthly Subscriptions it is unnecessary to say much. They stand in the same category with church-door collections and differ from them chiefly in these particulars, that the Church sends for them to the subscribers instead of the latter carrying them to the Church, and that the amount is less subject to variation. Subscriptions are also in general recorded, but this is a feature which, as we shall afterwards show, might with advantage be engrafted upon the plan of weekly Collections.

These are the modes in which money for ordinary congregational purposes is commonly raised. When extraordinary work has to be done, extraordinary methods are resorted to. For example, in the building of a new church, it is by no means unusual to devolve upon the minister the duty, or rather the task, of soliciting donations from wealthy persons outside of the congregation. When the calls thus to be made are confined to the district in which the future church is to stand, or when the work can be overtaken by the writing of a few letters, there may be no ground of reasonable objection to the adoption of this course, if the minister give his consent. But latterly a system pregnant with mischief, and threatening the most disastrous results to the Church, has grown up and attained an alarming development. The minister in an evil hour undertakes for the encouragement of his people to raise a certain proportion of the money required, or he is pressed to enlist himself in the service. Relinquishing his own proper post on the watch-tower of Zion, or, if not wholly relinquishing it, abstracting from the time and energy which the due performance of its duties requires, he takes up the business of "money raiser for ecclesiastical purposes," and sets out for one of our great commercial centres accompanied by the best wishes of his flock for his success and safe return. How far these wishes, so far as they concern the success of his mission, are gratified, depends on a variety of circumstances into which it is unnecessary to enter, except to mention that the one which often has least determining influence is the intrinsic merit of the cause. The applicant may return laden with the spoil of the great city, and picturing everything *couleur de rose* in his account of the reception accorded to him. Or, after many a weary journey over the hard and dusty streets, between piles of gigantic warehouses which mock him with their suggestions of untold wealth, he may return jaded, dispirited, and seriously injured for the time at least in his *morale*, having realised barely enough to cover the cost of his bitterly regretted expedition. Nor are the failures and consequent disappointments which sometimes occur, the greatest of the evils with which this practice is fraught. It is hurtful to the minister, to the congregation, and to those who are thus solicited. The minister cannot escape being more or less secularized by the part which he has to play. He cannot without injury to himself as well as to his people "leave the word of God to serve tables." His self-respect is exposed to great peril. With attention concentrated day after day, and often for a considerable period, upon the work of getting money, he runs a risk of occasionally forgetting that money in the hand of the Church is merely a means, and that it is far too dearly purchased by any sacrifice, however trifling, of those principles for the holding fast and holding forth of which, the Church exists. He is tempted to appeal to secondary and questionable motives, to bring side pressure to bear, and in other ways to leave the high and firm ground which should ever be occupied by the servant of the Lord; and to depart from that firm ground is to endanger the highest interests. A planned appeal to the interests or the humours of a man of the world may succeed in so far as it secures a cheque for so many guineas, but it may deepen rather than remove unfavourable impressions which he has formed respecting the reality of the work of the Church and the sincerity of those engaged in it. In such a case, who will contend that the pecuniary gain to the Church is any adequate compensation for the loss of moral power which it has sustained? The system is also hurtful to the congregation for which the aid is sought. It is deprived for a time of the benefit of that able and earnest ministry, which in most cases is incompatible with preoccupation of the mind with business of the kind in question, at a period when upon the ability and earnestness of the pulpit ministrations, success may very much depend. And lastly, it is a system which exposes a few nobly beneficent men to a multiplicity of calls, all of which they cannot respond to, and which it may yet give them sincere pain to set aside. In all our large cities there are men of known generosity, whose names are furnished to every one entering the field, and so it happens that the more a man gives, the more he is called upon to give. Many of the wealthiest escape these exactions, as they consider them, by resolutely refusing every application, and so making a reputation for "closeness" which protects them from many an inroad. It is also to be kept in mind that a considerable expense attends this mode of raising money, even when the utmost economy is practised. The cost of printing, postages, and travelling expenses is sometimes unpleasantly high, and donors give with full knowledge that five per cent., or perhaps even ten per cent., will have to be deducted from their donations before they are applied to their specific purpose.

In writing as he does on this topic, the writer has no intention to disparage the zeal, and what in many cases might be called the heroism, of ministers, who finding that the work in which they were engaged was great, that money was urgently needed, and that their own people with much willingness were yet unable to provide it, have undertaken to lead as it were a forlorn hope, and at the cost of much self-denial have successfully accomplished their voluntary task. The fault lies not with the weak congregations nor with their ministers, but with our whole system of giving for Church purposes. Weak congregations need help and have a right to it, but instead of their having to seek it in this beggarly fashion, it should be sent to them out of a rich and overflowing fund furnished by the consistent and constant liberality of the whole Church, and administered equitably and wisely. When the Church as a whole begins to respond to the urgent call of Christ, to give liberally, and to give as to Him, then these other and questionable forms of appeal will cease. A weak congregation will then be aided in its church-building or in its liquidation of debt, not in proportion to the persuasiveness in speech and manner of its minister, nor in proportion to the number and wealth of his personal friends, but in proportion to its merit and its need. Ministers will no longer be withdrawn from their sacred functions to perform the duties of clerks or canvassing agents. The hearts of many good and true Christians will be no longer grieved by having to inflict the pain of disappointment from sheer inability always to acknowledge claims which continue to multiply in exact proportion as they are acknowledged.

Another resort of weak congregations in times of necessity, and sometimes of congregations which cannot by any straining of language be called weak, is the holding of a Bazaar. Against this method of obtaining money for church purposes a widespread and growing feeling exists. The principle, that those who cannot give money should be allowed an opportunity of contributing their labour to Christ's cause, is perfectly sound; and it would not be difficult to construct an unimpeachable theory of Bazaars. But it must be admitted that, as they are generally conducted, many abuses exist in connection with them; and, unfortunately for their credit, we are constantly told that the practices complained of as objectionable are absolutely necessary to secure the pecuniary success. We do not enter further upon this somewhat difficult ground except to say that much advantage would result in many ways, were the temptation to have recourse to such methods removed, through the increased voluntary and direct offerings of the people.

A Course of Lectures on secular themes by the minister or by a series of lecturers, a charge being made for admission, is in some cases made a source of revenue. Or, the young people, uniting all their available musical skill, give a concert and devote the proceeds to one or other of the church schemes. Tea-meetings are held, tea being provided at the cost of a few generous ladies, and the money resulting from the sale of tickets is handed over to the treasurer. It is a very ungracious task to review critically these plans and labours of love. Such schemes suggested by loving hearts and executed by willing and active hands, have often served the immediate purpose which they were designed to serve. But questions do force themselves upon the minds of the observant and thoughtful, as to whether the raising of money by this "indirection" is worthy of the Christian Church, or compatible with a jealous regard to its strength and beauty; whether the money thus obtained has not been paid for ten times over, in loss of real nobility as well as of prestige, and whether the constant resort to such means does not jeopardise the income which is given directly to the treasury of the Lord "for Jesus' sake," and which, if it were only diligently and thoughtfully watched over and prayed over, would yield a larger amount than the combined returns from all such sources. The practical conclusion at which many arrive on pondering such questions is this, Let bazaars be held if they are desired, for the sale of the *bona fide* work of those who have only their work to bestow; let our young people have their musical soirees for recreation and amusement; let lectures be delivered for instruction; let congregations, on suitable occasions, take tea together; but let it no longer go forth to the world that the object of any of these gatherings is to raise, for the relief of the destitute Christian Church, funds, of which, through the neglect or the parsimony of her own children, she is in want. Instead of timidly laying snares in various forms for the unbelieving, the undevout, the selfish and the avaricious, and seeking to obtain money by guile, let there be a manly, direct, and faithful appeal to the conscience, the heart, and the intelligence of the Christian community. Instead of a dozen doubtful methods let there be one, strong in its simplicity, which shall alone achieve more than is achieved now by all the others combined, and which unlike them, instead of losing strength as the bloom of novelty departs, will grow mightier with the lapse of time, endearing itself to the hearts and intertwining with the habits of the people.

Before we leave this branch of our subject one lamentable consequence of the inadequacy of the Church's revenue calls for special notice,—the failure to provide a sufficient and honourable maintenance for all her ministers. No right is more strongly enforced in the Gospel than the right of those who preach the Gospel to live of the Gospel. Yet many able and faithful ministers of the Gospel live under a constant burden of care, if not of actual poverty, owing to the narrowness of the income with which the Church provides them. This is a manifest injustice to the servants of Christ, but the loss does not fall most heavily on the immediate sufferers. The Church itself loses immensely more. "A scandalous maintenance makes a scandalous ministry," Matthew Henry has wisely observed. It is not possible that a mind harassed with care, and depressed by poverty, can yield the rich fruits of study and meditation in equal profusion with a mind at ease and free to devote itself to its proper work.

The poverty of the manse tells also upon the number and social status of candidates for the ministry. Young men of fair talents, and with ordinarily good prospects in life, in many cases decline the ministry because of the sorrowful prospect which it holds out to them with regard to temporal support. It may be retorted that those who desire the work for its own sake will not be deterred by such a consideration from entering upon it, and that they only are really called to it. As a reply to this weak defence of a bad system, we quote the following words from an admirable lay writer on this subject. "It may perhaps be said that young men of talent, if they feel *called* to preach the Gospel, ought to devote themselves to the preaching of the Gospel whether they have a prospect of being adequately supported or not. I doubt this; I dispute this. Men may feel called to devote themselves to the *preaching of the Gospel* who do not feel called to devote themselves to *semi-starvation.* They may determine to preach the Gospel, but they may determine to preach it as Paul preached it. They may work with their own hands; they may devote themselves to some secular calling that they may make for themselves an adequate maintenance; and they may preach the Gospel as what are now called "local preachers." But then, the churches, in such cases, would not accept them as settled pastors. If, then, churches are to have settled pastors equal in point of talents and attainments to the requirements of the times, they must seriously consider the question of *materially increasing* ministerial pay." Besides this, it must be remembered that it is one thing "to suffer affliction *with* the people of God," and another thing to suffer injustice at their hands. Many a noble Christian man, who in the service of his Master knows both how to be abased and how to abound, to be full and to be hungry, to abound and to suffer need, and who would be prepared to submit to any privations necessarily attending that service, recoils from the thought of a poverty occasioned by the selfishness or inconsiderateness of those among whom he is expected daily to break the bread of life. There is a poverty of God's servants, and there are privations endured by them, that redound to the glory of His grace. There are also privations and poverty that redound only to the shame of the Church. To be willing to choose the one, and yet indignantly to spurn the other, may be equally the part of a sincere, divinely-called evangelist.

Thus we bring to a close this rapid and necessarily

very cursory survey of our existing methods of giving and their results. We have sought to show that these methods are more or less faulty in principle, and that in practice they fail to evoke the liberality of the Church in any measure at all corresponding to the greatness either of the obligation under which it lies, or of the work which it is called to do. They are unjust, inasmuch as they often fall with equal incidence on rich and poor. From their multiplicity and indirectness, they are wasteful of the time and energy of those by whom they are administered; and from the irregularities and inequalities which they favour, they often weaken the moral and spiritual power of the Church while replenishing its treasury. The state of things which we have been describing exists, we believe, in most of our congregations, and among a majority of the members of the Church. It would be unfair, however, not to add that a very considerable minority, dissatisfied with past results, and tracing their unsatisfactoriness to the erroneous views and methods which have prevailed, have sought and discovered that more excellent way which it will be our business in the next chapter to indicate, and are now walking in it with growing comfort, joy, and usefulness.

With gladness, also, we are daily reminded that there is an increasing number of capitalists, merchants, and manufacturers, who realise the responsibility which comes with riches, and who consider themselves under deepest obligations to take an active and considerable part in promoting the well-being of their employed and of the community. These men are the glory of our country, and if their example is emulated, as we have ground to hope that it will be, by the rising generation, calamities which otherwise seem imminent may be averted, and another and yet brighter day of power and pre-eminence may dawn for Great Britain.

CHAPTER VII.

A MORE EXCELLENT WAY.

Every new movement in the Church, whether of revival or reform, has been preceded by increased diligence and earnestness in the study of the Scriptures. Their inexhaustible supply ministers to all healthy and strong spiritual life, and when torpor has seized upon the Church, and it is languishing in a state of declension and decay, it is from them that the impulses and stirrings of a new life come. "The words that I speak unto you, they are spirit and they are life." When earnest Christians find that they cannot accept the self-complacent view which the Church too often takes of the work it is doing, and of the sacrifice it is making, for its Lord,—it being only too manifest on inquiry, that, notwithstanding much loud vaunting and self-congratulation, the givings are such as it should rather be ashamed of, and the work overtaken in the great field of the world so small that it may well occasion deep sadness and humiliation,—the next step is to search the Scriptures in order to discover why these things are so. The lively oracles of truth must be consulted, and answers sought to such questions as the following :— "Has the Church an adequate sense of its responsibility on the one hand, and on the other, of its privilege, in having addressed to it the high calling of God? Have its labours been truly 'abundant'? Has its giving been commensurate either with its obligations or with the urgent requirements of God's work? Have its methods of providing for the Lord's treasury been adopted in literal obedience to God's instructions as we find them in the Scriptures, or have they at least been in accordance with their spirit?" To these questions, an unprejudiced comparison of the existing state of things with the precepts and ideals of Scripture must surely result in the reply of an emphatic "No!" And if we proceed to turn over the sacred pages in hopes of finding a method of church finance there indicated, our search will not be fruitless. The New Testament does indicate such a method, one stamped with the divine approval, and strongly recommended to, if not enjoined upon, the ancient Churches. It is true that the statement of it is brief, that it is not expressed in legal phraseology, such as Moses used, that it seems to occur incidentally, and is neither prefaced nor elaborately illustrated, but it is not the less clear, precise, and authoritative. It is to be found in the First Epistle to the Corinthians, chap. xvi., vv. 1, 2. " Now, concerning the collection for the saints, as I have given order to the Churches of Galatia, even so do ye. Upon the first day of the week, let every one of you lay by him in store as God hath prospered him, that there be no gatherings when I come."

Money was much needed by the Church at this time, and in these words we have the inspired Apostle's instructions how to raise it. He was not recommending the Corinthians to give this method a trial by way of experiment; it was already in operation under his supervision in the Churches of Galatia. And it was not in the form of a suggestion which they might or might not adopt at will that he submitted it to them. He had given "order" to the Galatians respecting it, and to the Corinthians he addresses an unqualified imperative, having all the force of the apostolical authority with which he had been invested, "so do ye." This, then, is the more excellent way of church finance. It is God's own way. How blessed would the Church be, walking in it! Her path, then, like that of the just, would be "as the shining light, shining more and more unto the perfect day."

But this method, besides having the authority of Scripture, commends itself, as might have been expected from its origin, to common sense and good feeling, and holds in it rich promise of better days for the Church, and consequently for the world. We propose to look at it somewhat closely from this point of view, and for the sake of order we shall take up in succession its salient features.

1. *Every one to give.* We find from the superscription of the Epistle, that the writer is addressing "the Church of God which is at Corinth, those who are sanctified in Christ Jesus, called to be saints, with all that in every place call upon the name of Jesus Christ our Lord, both theirs and ours." The words "every one of you," include, therefore, all the members of the Church. Neither the young nor the poor are exempted. Those who have received anything of the Lord are required to render an account of it, and to bestow a portion in His service. The reasonableness of this requirement will appear when we remember that giving is an act of worship, and that it is also an occasion of blessing to the giver. No one is excused from rendering homage to the Divine Majesty. "Unto Me every knee shall bow, every tongue shall swear." God is the Maker of the poor as of the rich, and to rich and poor alike His will is intimated, "Bring an offering and come before Him, worship the Lord in the beauty of holiness." And if God does not dispense with the gifts of the poor, neither can the poor afford to dispense with the blessing which rests upon every devout and faithful giver. The hardships and trials of their

lot would press heavily indeed, were it not for the relief obtained by accepting the gracious invitation "Cast thy burden upon the Lord," and God is nearer to none than to the poor who sincerely love and trust Him and hearken to His word. Those who make their poverty an excuse for giving nothing, are wronging not God but themselves, and they are more likely to remain poor than those who in the deepest poverty do not cease to honour God. The young are included also. Of course, where there is no income there can be no storing of the Lord's portion, but most even of the younger children have small sums of money occasionally at their disposal, and they should be encouraged to exercise self-denial in order that they may be able in outward act, as well as in thought, to remember their Creator in the days of their youth. It is a common practice when children are setting out for church, to hand them money to place in the collection plate, and it is perhaps better that they should be the bearers of another's bounty than that they should go empty-handed. But it would be better still to entrust them with small sums of money as their own, and to encourage the freewill offering of a portion of this little capital. The child who thus gives of his own, and makes a sacrifice to be able to do it, personally renders homage to God, advances his cause, and at the same time lays the foundation of the character of the faithful steward.

Sometimes the question is asked, Should ministers be expected to give? The answer might well be, Why should they not give? The same worship is required of them as of their flock. They have a right to the same privilege of lending to the Lord, and they equally need the blessing associated with giving. Under the old economy the Levites who received tithes from the other tribes gave tithes to the priests, and the priests offered for themselves. In liberal and cheerful giving, as in all other duties, it becomes the pastor to be an example to his flock. Avarice and selfishness are never more repulsive than when exhibited by a professed minister of Jesus Christ. The manifest insincerity of one who discourses on the reality and the greatness of the Redeemer's Kingdom, and who refuses to sacrifice a few luxuries or comforts so as to be able to take his part in advancing it, have often pained earnest and thoughtful Christians, and afforded a welcome opportunity to the scoffer.

The question has also been asked, Should irreligious men be asked to contribute to the cause of religion? As long as we preserve simplicity and candour in stating the case, and appeal directly to whatever good principles and benevolent impulses may exist in the hearts of those whom we are addressing, we may not only with consistency and safety, but with great advantage, from every point of view, seek the help of all in the furtherance of the Church's work. An appeal thus made to an irreligious man would be virtually a preaching of the Gospel to him, and that in a practical form which might be more suggestive than any other. But to preserve such simplicity and candour perfectly, in approaching ungodly and irreligious men with such an appeal, demands both force of character and singleness of purpose, and where these are not possessed, the temptation to compromise and *indirection* may be irresistible, and much harm may thus be done. From approaches of this nature, men of the world naturally conclude that the Church has reversed its ancient policy, "We seek not yours but you," and even when they give, they give half-heartedly, not as to the Lord but as to men.

2. *Givings to be stored.* This is the essential feature

of the apostolic method, and we cannot too much admire the wisdom which appointed it. Money is not to be given directly from a private purse to the various objects which commend themselves to our approval. We are to lay by whatever we dedicate to God, keeping it apart from personal property as being no longer our own, and when suitable occasions arise, we are to disburse it just as we would the bounty of another, of which we had been made stewards. The advantages gained by this severance of the act of dedication to God from the act of dispensing what has been thus dedicated are many and great. It enables us to keep an account as it were with conscience, and so to avoid the sin and shame of withholding more than is due. Those whose habit is to give from a private purse, and to keep no record of such outlays, generally form an exaggerated estimate of the sum total of their benefactions. It admits of the solemn consecration of God's portion. The arrangement being to present it at a set time, prayer and suitable meditation may accompany this presentation, and so the blessedness of giving may be greatly enhanced. It relieves from all doubts as to whether or not we are able, without injustice to ourselves and others, to contribute on any particular occasion, seeing we have only to refer to the amount we have in hand as the stewards of the Lord's portion for a settlement of this question. Decision and promptitude thus take the place of hesitation, and we neither run the risk of refusing to assist a worthy cause from an unfounded misgiving as to our ability, nor are we reproached by conscience when, the balance available being exhausted, we cease to give till the next period of replenishment puts more at our disposal. Money is more willingly and cheerfully given when it is taken from a fund provided for the purpose than when it has to be withdrawn from capital, or taken from a private purse in the midst of the hurry and cares of business. And lastly there is the advantage to which Paul refers when he expresses a desire that there should be no gatherings when he came to Corinth to receive the collection. Where givings are stored they are always ready for bestowal as God may direct. The acts of beneficence which those who give without system resolve upon, are often left unperformed when the time for performance comes, not because of any change in the mind of the intending donor, but simply because the money which was to have been forthcoming, has meanwhile been thoughtlessly expended in other ways. Such mishaps can never befall the Lord's portion when periodically stored. "The secret of the Lord is with them that fear him," and those who do not possess this particular secret of power and willinghood, are often surprised at the promptitude and liberality with which men, whom they know to be comparatively poor, respond to almost every call made upon them in the name of religion or charity.

3. *Giving to be in proportion as God has prospered.* This is the only equitable principle upon which to proceed in determining the question of How much? in Christian giving. The amount is to be according to the ability of the giver. An assessment based upon any other principle than this is manifestly, and often in the highest degree, unjust. To give practical effect to this injunction two things must be done. Each one must determine what proportion of his income he is prepared to consecrate, and the amount of the income itself must be ascertained. The question of proportion has already received attention from us, and need not be entered into again at any great length. A few things, however, must be said. The principle which the government of this

country has acted upon in the imposition of the Income Tax, namely, that the smaller incomes should not only be chargeable with a smaller amount of taxation, but with a smaller proportion, is fairly applicable here. The smaller incomes are very largely expended in providing the necessaries of life. The larger incomes are mainly expended in the purchase of luxuries. Just as the act of Sir Philip Sidney in handing to a dying soldier the cup of cold water, with which he was about to allay his own burning thirst, stands greatly higher on the scale of generosity than the profuse hospitality of the city magnate who entertains his guests with the costliest wines, so the poor man giving say a tenth of his income, may exhibit a loftier spirit of self-denial than the wealthy man in giving a fifth or even a third. If the apostolic principle of equal distribution is to be honoured, " I mean not that other men be eased and ye burdened, but by an equality," the proportion must increase as we ascend in the scale of wealth. This has been very far from being so in the past. As a rule the poor have given in much larger proportion than the rich, notwithstanding that the gifts of the poor often necessitate a retrenchment in the expenditure on necessaries, while the gifts of the rich affect only their luxuries, perhaps not even their luxuries, but only the amount of their balance at the bank. The failure to give in proportion as God has prospered, and the substitution for this divine method of the human one, of giving in the smallest proportion which conscience or regard to public opinion will admit of, and only to such demands as are loudly pressed, has been the chief cause of the wretched insufficiency of the total givings of the Church and of the country. When our rich men begin to measure their obligations not by the gifts of their poor neighbours, nor by the number and clamancy of the causes which "come" to them for help, but solely by the extent to which God has prospered them, and by the vast and constant demands of His glorious kingdom, then a new era will be inaugurated in the history of the Church of Christ at home and abroad.

The proportion to be given must be determined by each one for himself in the court of conscience. We have seen that, in Scripture times, Abraham and Jacob gave a tenth, the devout Jews probably a fifth, Zacchæus the penitent a half, and the poor widow at the temple gate all her living that she had. Nowhere in Scripture do we read of a less proportion being offered than a tenth. Idolaters in many lands give a tenth to the service of their gods. It is surely not too much to say that in no case should the offering of a Christian, in this nineteenth century and in this land of privilege and of power, fall below the proportion which was the *minimum* in the twilight ages of Judaism, and which is even now accorded by the votaries of error and superstition.

The proportion to be stored as God's having been fixed, the amount of the income is next to be ascertained. When it consists of a stated yearly salary or a weekly wage, no difficulty exists; and even when it is derived from business or a profession, the difficulty arising from the uncertain amount of the profits in the year's transactions may be overcome by taking the average of the past three or four years as the basis of calculation. The impossibility of precisely estimating one's profits, and the general uncertainties of business, are not unfrequently pleaded by those engaged in mercantile pursuits as an excuse for not giving systematically. The excuse, however, is devoid of real force, for the amount of the income must be furnished to the Commissioners of Income Tax, and if the difficulty is surmounted in the one case, it cannot be insuperable in the other.

4. *Giving to be weekly and on the Christian Sabbath.* Giving being an act of worship, it is appropriate that it should have assigned for its exercise that day which is specially dedicated to the service of God. Being a token of gratitude, it is meet that the gift should be rendered on the day which commemorates those two great works of Creation and Redemption, in which God's goodness to man is most conspicuously displayed. Being an expression of interest in our fellow-men, it is most consistently referred to the day of rest, when the mind, free from the hurry and anxiety of business, has leisure to rise into calmer regions, and to meditate on such themes as the brotherhood of the human family, the duty of bearing one another's burdens, and the blessedness of that coming time when the Kingdom of God, as delineated by Christ, shall be established in the hearts of all. Most wisely, therefore, has the Church been instructed to select for the time of its offering the first day of the week. In these days there exists in many hearts a longing after ritual, a craving for outward acts as expressive of the inner life. Here is a simple rite which may be so performed as to conduce, far more than the most gorgeous decorations or elaborate ceremonial, to the development of faith and love. The Sabbath has often been found by God's people a resting-place between earth and heaven. By the solemn and prayerful consecration of our substance to God on this day, we establish another connecting link between the seen and the unseen, the temporal and the eternal. We spiritualise our secular business, and provide a practical expression for our spiritual aspirations. From that weekly render-

ing of an account to God, the man of business carries away hallowed impressions and impulses which regulate all his business relations, the professional man proceeds under the same influences to his engagements, the labouring man to his toil. And having been sustained and blessed during the week, they all return again on the Sabbath, as the Samaritan who had been healed returned, to give glory to God, and to seek a renewal of sweet and strength-ministering communion. What more effectual safeguard could be erected against the dangers of worldliness, excessive love of money, absorption in self, and engrossment with the secular and material, than is to be found in this practice. How completely does it provide against the insidious growth of that hypocrisy, which, when it is fully developed, is so hateful to God and man, the hypocrisy of indulging in high-sounding religious phraseology, ostentatious profession and magnificent promise, while refusing to touch with the little finger any of the real burdens of Christian work and sacrifice.

Besides the propriety of the day fixed for giving, the frequency enjoined is a noteworthy feature of the method. *Every week* the offering is to be brought to the store. Thus a constant sense of dependence is maintained, as the giver is reminded at brief intervals of those obligations which are too readily forgotten, and which we are specially prone to forget in a season of prosperity.

Such are the distinctive features of the apostolic method. But besides the passage in which they are detailed, there are many instructions and exhortations bearing on this duty of giving, scattered throughout the New Testament, which have a special reference to this method, and which show still more clearly its admirable sufficiency as a means of grace to the giver, and as a mode of supplying the need of the Church. Giving is set before us as a channel through which may flow expressions of our gratitude. "The administration of this service is abundant by many thanksgivings unto God." It is shown that it is a proof of sincerity, and that it not only manifests but fosters that virtue. "By the experiment of this ministration they glorify God for your professed subjection unto the Gospel of Christ." It is declared to be a source of the purest happiness. "I have showed you all things how that so labouring, ye ought to support the weak, and to remember the words of the Lord Jesus, how he said, It is more blessed to give than to receive." It is assumed that the method contributes to that cheerfulness in giving, which is essential to its being well-pleasing in the sight of God. "Every man according as he purposeth in his heart so let him give, not grudgingly or of necessity, for God loveth a cheerful giver." It is recommended as encouraging us to give from the simple desire to do good, and as obviating any sense on the one hand of having sustained a loss, or on the other of having incurred an irksome obligation. "I thought it necessary to exhort the brethren that they would go before unto you and make up beforehand your bounty, whereof ye had notice before, that the same might be ready as a matter of bounty and not as of covetousness."

Let us now see how this method, enjoined thus strictly upon ancient Christians, would meet the exigences of modern life. Let us suppose the case of one who, from considering the present unsatisfactory state of Church finance has been led to make inquiries, and who,—having discovered in the Scriptures a method of giving, of which he is assured that were it to come into universal operation, it would effect a complete and salutary revolution, —has resolved whatever others may continue to do, personally to adopt this method. He decides to make full proof of it, and accordingly he conforms carefully to the spirit of the various Apostolic injunctions and recommendations respecting it. He resolves that in giving henceforth, he will give in obedience to the command of God, and not as yielding to the solicitation of men. His giving will be an act of worship, an acknowledgment of dependence and obligation, an expression of gratitude. It will also be a practical outcome from his interest in the welfare of his fellow-men, and a contribution to the advancement of the Redeemer's Kingdom among them. He will give a fixed proportion of his income, and in determining that proportion he will ask the guidance of the Holy Spirit, keeping in view the unspeakable greatness of the works to be advanced, the responsibility laid upon all to take part in them to the utmost of their ability, the blessed reward of those who are good and faithful servants, and the doom of the unfaithful. He will not set aside the amount thus fixed thoughtlessly; but he will make the offering an occasion of prayer and meditation, and he will find both time and circumstances favourable to these, selecting as he does the Sabbath day for the discharge of this duty in conformity with the Scripture rule. Every Sabbath day he will thus renew a covenant with God, similar to that which Jacob entered into at Bethel. "Of all that Thou shalt give me, I will surely give the tenth unto Thee." His whole spiritual life will find in this observance a delightful channel in which it will flow with ever fuller tide. Spiritual Christianity and Practical Christianity, Faith and Works, Holiness unto the Lord, and Helpfulness towards men will thus be combined, and a higher type of devout and manly religion will be reached.

Christian families, in which this practice of laying by

in store is observed, are schools of faith and trust, of love and obedience. As the children witness Sabbath after Sabbath the practical proof of the sincerity and strength of a father's and a mother's faith, and as they themselves occasionally or regularly take part in the offering, they acquire deep and thorough convictions of the being and goodness of God, they are habituated to regard religion as a real thing, than which nothing is more real, they learn to associate it with sublime ideas of duty and of hope, and they are prepared to be governed by it as they play a manly part in the life that lies before them. The power of the concrete and spectacular to impress children is well known. Early experiences indelibly impress themselves, and their effects are traceable in character and disposition, long after the experiences themselves have lost their original power to impress. To be present at a family gathering, convened for the purpose of intelligently and solemnly consecrating a portion of the family income to the service of God in the great conflict, ever in progress, of good against evil, would be an interesting experience to any Christian man or woman, but it is not probable that it would of itself deeply affect the character of the mature observer. It is very different however with the children. And other circumstances being equally favourable, we would be justified in expecting to find them growing up men of faith and zeal, scorners of compromise with evil, ever ready to come to the help of the Lord against the mighty, to make sacrifices and to endure hardness as good soldiers of Jesus Christ. And if such were the educating influence of this practice, would not the wise and good Christian parents by whom it was adopted bequeath to their children, in the Christian heroism, the Christian sympathies, and the habits of self-control and self-denial which they had thus formed and fostered, a far more precious legacy than a fortune equal to the accumulated offerings of a lifetime a thousand times told.

Before passing from the consideration of this practice it is right that we should notice some of the views and arguments of those who either refuse to adopt it themselves, or object to its being urged upon the Church. Many profess to be opposed to it because of its novelty. To this charge it is sufficient to reply that the method is novel only in the sense in which the doctrine of justification by faith preached by Luther in the beginning of the sixteenth century was novel. If the Scriptures be the standard of correct and authoritative practice as well as of sound doctrine, then it is to our existing methods, and not to the one which it is proposed to substitute for them, that the stigma of "novelty" attaches.

Others object to the requirement of a fixed proportion of the income. "This," say they, "interferes with, if it does not destroy the sense of freedom. Under such a system the offering ceases to have the character of a voluntary service, and assumes that of an obligation." There is an ambiguity in the use of these words "voluntary" and "freedom" which it may be well to remove, as the difficulty which is made to hinge upon them will then be easily disposed of. If by "freedom," is meant the absence of external constraint, direct or indirect, then all giving ought to be free,—"not of necessity, but as every man purposes in his heart." But if by "freedom," is meant the absence of the self-imposed restraint of good resolutions, then neither in giving nor in any other duty is it desirable to be free. In truth, this is not to be free, but to be governed by caprice and momentary impulse, a subjection which often deteriorates into the worst form of bondage. "He is the freeman whom the truth makes free." And he is the freeman whose actions are in accordance with the dictates of reason and conscience, and not subject to the fierce control of passion or the tyranny of whim. But why should the objection to a systematic mode of meeting our obligations be raised only when the claims of religion and philanthropy are in question? Are men of business blamed for cultivating business habits, and laying down rules for times and modes of payment, which they observe themselves and which they expect those with whom they deal punctually to observe? Are we to be commended for paying to the uttermost farthing, and within the prescribed period, our rents, taxes, shopkeepers' bills, doctors' and lawyers' accounts, and are we to be blamed for insisting on the duty of a correspondingly regular and systematic acknowledgment of the claims which God has upon us? "But there is a difference," the objector sometimes replies, "between the accounts referred to and the claims of religion. Those are legal debts, these are merely moral obligations." We accept this distinction, but the drawing of it reveals the real nature of the objection. The claims of religion are not legally, they are *merely* morally binding! The objection then comes from those who do not recognise in moral obligation a power which binds the conscience of the good man far more firmly than legal enactments. Those who thus demur, to be candid, should object not to being asked to contribute systematically what they owe to the cause of God, but to being asked to contribute at all as a matter of obligation. To such cavillers it is not the excellence of any particular method of meeting the obligation, but the existence of the obligation itself, which we need to make plain. Their objection in short is the old and common one, "I pray thee have me excused."

A third class have a difficulty which is really the same as that just disposed of, though it is presented in a different form. "We are not to dedicate a tenth merely," say they, "or even a fifth or a half, we are to dedicate all." This sounds like the utterance of a geneous and heroic heart. But when we come to inquire into the meaning of the phrase "dedicating to God," as employed by these persons, we find that it is used of all expenditure indiscriminately; what is for purely personal ends as well as what is for religion and charity. They dedicate money, they say, when they part with it for any useful and honourable purpose upon which they can ask God's blessing. "What I expend in supporting and educating my children, that I consider dedicated to God," says one. "What I spend on my library, or on the embellishment of my house, and thus indirectly in the improvement of my condition, that I regard as dedicated to God," says another. To this mode of treating the subject grave exception must be taken Money paid as an equivalent for value received in substance by ourselves or our families, in whatever form, is not in the Scriptural sense dedicated to God. If the matter is wholly one of the meaning and applicability of words, it is of small moment; but it is to be feared that this cloak of universal dedication is too often used to conceal the condemning disparity of the portion dedicated to the support of religion and that "dedicated" to self.

"There is no command to give a tenth," say a fourth class. We do not assert that there is such a command in the New Testament. But the Old Testament, not less than the New, is to be regarded by the Church. The assertion that holy men of old wrote as they were moved by the Holy Ghost applied to the Old Testament. And both the command to give a tenth, and the practice of giving it, are there very plainly recorded. Under the new dispensation our obligations are greater, as partakers of higher privileges and more glorious light; there is a more powerful motive to liberality in the constraining love of Christ; and the requirements of the service of Christ are greater, as the Church is no longer national or territorial but has a commission to go into all the world. The question then is this, Can we consistently admit the authority of the Scriptures and give less than a tenth? and the settlement of it may fairly be left to the conscience of any sincere and earnest Christian.

"Liberality measured out thus exactly and with such ceremony will speedily degenerate into formalism," say others. "More may be given but it will be given in a dull mechanical way. The life and heartiness of giving on impulse will be lost." This is a specious objection, but a little consideration will show that it is devoid of force. The danger of formalism no doubt exists, but it exists equally in other departments of religious service. We do not cease to attend the sanctuary, or to keep holy the Sabbath, because church-going and Sabbath observance often degenerate into formalism. And with regard to the other mode of stating the objection, while it is true that acts performed frequently and regularly are necessarily unattended by the excitement, and consequently may not have the zest, of novelty, it is to be remembered that a habitual serenity and happiness are of far greater value than any number of transient flashes of joy, and that the abiding satisfaction which is valuable because of its bearing on the character, is promoted far more by systematic than by spasmodic giving.

There is just one other objection to which we shall refer, and it is not an objection to the system proposed, but merely to the feasibility of its universal adoption.

"It may do for the rich, but not for the poor. To ask a labouring man with a large family, for example, to contribute in any proportion of his income approaching a tenth would be unreasonable, to say the least." This language is very plausible, certainly, and has the appearance of good sense and practical wisdom. We are persuaded, nevertheless, that it proceeds from that wisdom of the world which is foolishness with God. We have already stated our conviction that God requires and rejoices in the gifts of the poor, and that He is so faithful in His promises to bless those who acknowledge Him in this way, that to debar the poor from giving systematically is to wrong them. If God blesses and accepts the two mites which the widow casts into the treasury, these being all her living, who will raise his hand to thrust back the offerings of the poor? He who does so is acting no friendly part to his client, and he is greatly dishonouring God. He virtually says to the poor, "Take back your money; it will do you more good than the blessing of the Almighty. Purchase with it food and raiment; they are of more value to you than the consciousness of a loyal and trusting heart. The blessedness of giving is a luxury beyond your reach, and to which you must not aspire. God has not chosen the poor of this world for this service. Go back to your family, and allow those who are abler than you are to serve." Hard words—such as if expressed would have elicited a stern rebuke from the Master. Christ had a deep acquaintance with poverty. He was Himself poor, and He lived among the poor. He knew all the peculiar difficulties, dangers, temptations, hardships, and sorrows, as He knew also the peculiar joys, incident to their lot. And as the result of his experience and insight he said —" Blessed be ye poor, for yours is the kingdom of

God." Now, what is it to possess the Kingdom, if it be not to have the disposition and the ability to do good, to give, to lend, looking for nothing again, and thus to be the children of the Highest? Are the poor specially the heirs of the Kingdom, and are they to be excluded from one of the most precious privileges of the Kingdom? Did some officious individual encounter those ten lepers that were cleansed, of whom we read, and by forcible representation convince nine of them that their taking the trouble to return to thank Christ and give glory to God was foolish and even reprehensible, that the Physician had not required it, that he was probably too much occupied to receive them again, that their time was valuable now that they were restored to health, and that the sooner they got home to set about their work the better it would be for themselves and for their families? We are not informed: but such an interposition would have been an exact type of the conduct of those who, esteeming themselves wiser than God, seek to intercept the gifts of the poor on their way to God's treasury.

Looking at the objection from another point of view, we might remind the objectors that there are few of the irreligious poor who do not tax themselves at a much higher rate than one tenth for the gratification of hurtful tastes and passions. Happy would it be for many a wretched family if not a tenth but a half of the weekly earnings were given to any purpose, so that they might no longer be expended in the purchase of degradation and misery.

But the most conclusive answer remains to be returned, and it is that many of the poor do contribute a tenth or more already, and this often without any resolution to dedicate a fixed proportion. The following instance, known to the writer, may be given as an example. A mechanic earning thirty-two shillings weekly, and having a wife and four children to support, gives one shilling to the church weekly offering, sixpence weekly to a church-building fund, five shillings monthly towards the support of an aged mother, not less than sixpence weekly to various charities, besides contributing to religious purposes, in sundry collections and other ways, an amount not to be reckoned at less than twenty shillings per annum. Here we have a working man, without the guidance of system, contributing more than one-tenth of his small income to the purposes of beneficence and religion. Many such cases are to be found in humble life, and in no case are these noble givers losers by their liberality. He who clothes the lily and sustains the sparrow will not suffer his children, who trust in Him and obey His word, to lack or suffer hunger. "I have been young, and now am old," says the Psalmist, "yet have I not seen the righteous forsaken, nor his seed begging bread." Let those with whom we are now dealing, instead of rushing to the front as the self-constituted apologists of the poor in this matter of giving, make a few inquiries and a few calculations, and the result will be in many cases that, instead of standing up to apologise, they will be seen to retire in haste, confounded by revelations of a liberality so far exceeding their own.

A fund having thus been provided, the questions arise, In what manner, to what objects, and in what measure, is it to be applied? A wide field is here opened up for the exercise of Christian intelligence. The Lord's portion is limited, and as it will not bear too frequent or too extensive draughts, thought must be given in order that it may be laid out to the best advantage.

Much will, of course, depend upon the position and circumstances of the giver, and the relations to the Church and society which he finds himself occupying. Claims may be so numerous and so pressing that it may sometimes be difficult to decide which shall have precedence. But a loving heart, guided by a sober judgment, will come to right conclusions. These were the blessings which the Apostle sought for his Philippian converts—"I pray that your love may abound yet more and more in knowledge and in all judgment, that ye may approve things that are excellent."

There are two principles laid down in Scripture upon which it is our duty to proceed in all allocation. Giving is to be 'for Jesus' sake,' and worthy objects in our own neighbourhood are to have the first claim. The cup of cold water, the giving of which is to meet so great a reward, must have been given "in the name of a disciple," that is 'for Jesus' sake.' Peter, in conferring the boon of health on the poor cripple at the beautiful gate of the temple, used the words, "In the name of Jesus Christ of Nazareth, rise up and walk." We can scarcely assign any limit to the blessed results that would follow the universal observance of this rule. If, in giving, every one were to give from the simple motive of love to Christ, and a desire to promote his glory and the accomplishment of His work, and if he were not only to be conscious of this himself, but without ostentation or formality to make it apparent to others, then each act of giving would be a powerful preaching of Christ, and an enforcement of his claims to the love, reverence, and worship of all mankind. Many are deterred from confessing Christ in the performance of this duty by an unworthy pusillanimity, others by a conscientious fear of falling into the hypocrisy of too favourably representing their motives, in which they are conscious of a mingling of the questionable with the disinterested, while the majority fail from want of thought, and an inadequate sense of personal responsibility. But surely there is no command which the Christian should be more ready to obey, than that which bids him bring his gracious Master to the front and exalt his name above every name. "Whatsoever ye do, in word or deed, do all in the name of the Lord Jesus." How greatly Christ would be glorified, and his claims to the homage of every human heart pressed upon the world, if the language, the tone, and the manner of His people in giving were such as to lead the world to say—not "How liberal," or "How lavish," "How good-hearted," or "How foolish these Christians are!" but "How deep and strong is the hold which He whom they call their Saviour has taken of these men!" The Christian thus giving, would preach not himself but Christ Jesus the Lord, and himself the servant of all for Jesus' sake. Nor would the advantage of giving expressly in the name of Jesus be confined to the deep and salutary impression which would thus be made on the world. The Christian men and women to whom it might fall to receive, or convey, or redistribute offerings thus made, would be refreshed in spirit, lifted up to a higher faith and a clearer perception of the true ends of their work, and inspired with greater zeal in pursuing them. Thus the giver would immeasurably enhance the value of his gift, making it not only at its ultimate destination, but in its course, the means of precious spiritual blessing.

The other principle mentioned was the priority of local claims. The preaching of the gospel was by express command of Christ to begin *at Jerusalem*. The word *especially* occurs several times in the epistles of Paul, to indicate the duty of discriminating among modes of service, and of selecting those which lie nearest to us. The reasonableness of this order, and the great benefit to society which would attend its observance, are so manifest as to need no illustration. The town in which we reside, the denomination to which we are attached, the congregation with which we are connected, the neighbours among whom we live, have such special claims. We are not required, however, to apply all to local or denominational purposes, however important and necessary these may be. And it is often found that those whose charity begins at home, and is richest there, are the most liberal in dispensing abroad.

The claim which takes precedence of all is that of the Church. The support of the gospel ministry, so carefully provided for, so strenuously insisted on, in the New Testament, demands the first, if not the largest portion of what has been consecrated to the service of God. The Christian Church is "the Church of the living God, the pillar and ground of the truth," and faithful ministers are its strength and glory. It is of first importance, therefore, that an adequate provision be made for their maintenance in such a position, and in such freedom from earthly cares, as may be most favourable to the successful prosecution of their work.

When the practice of laying by in store for God's service is largely adopted, it is very easy to substitute for the unequal, complex, and cumbrous methods of raising congregational funds in ordinary use, one simple and efficient system yielding really satisfactory results. We refer to the weekly offering for church purposes which has been introduced into many Churches. Under this system there are no seat-rents, no collected subscriptions, no special collections, and there need be no money-making concerts, lectures, or bazaars. Seats may be appropriated as at present, but whatever is paid, is paid not in the form of rent, but as a direct contribution towards the expenses of the Church, including the stipend of the minister. Every one is expected to give something, to give an amount in proportion to ability, and to give that amount weekly. The offerings are generally enclosed in numbered envelopes, in order that they may be duly acknowledged by the secretary at the end of the quarter or half-year, and that so all things may be done decently and in order. An efficient and pains-taking secretary, acting in conjunction with a small committee, is able to overtake all the necessary work. Every one is allowed to contribute "as he purposes in his heart." There is no undue or indirect pressure, and consequently there is no room for grudging. Appeals are made only to the grand motives of love to the Lord, interest in the prosperity of his Church, and desire for its extension. When the system is fairly introduced, and the work intelligently conducted, the duty of laying by in store on the Sabbath being at the same time explained and enforced occasionally from the pulpit, the results have been most encouraging. Greater alacrity and cheerfulness in giving, deeper interest in Church work, and an increased spirituality in the tone of the congregation, are everywhere testified to. At the annual meeting of a Congregational church in London (Dr Raleigh's), it was stated that the income yielded by this system amounted to £6000, and that since its adoption all the schemes of the Church were amply supplied with funds, whereas under the old system of collected subscriptions, they were constantly in debt. A congregation in Melbourne (Rev. Mr Henderson's), by means of the freewill offering, raised £16,000 in two years for the building of a new church. In the report for 1873 of Richmond Chapel, Salford, we read, " In 1872 pew rents and weekly offerings together raised £768. Weekly offerings alone in 1873 realised £958, an increase of £190." These instances illustrate the working of the system in wealthy congregations, and in those which may be considered well to do. The following was given by Dr M'Auslane of Finsbury as a specimen of its perfect adaptability to the poorest. It is the case of a Church in Ireland, no member of which, with one exception, is worth half-a-crown beyond his or her weekly income. "One member with wife and three children contributes 1s. weekly. A second with wife and five children contributes 1s. 6d. weekly. A mother and her four daughters contribute 2s. 6d. weekly. Four factory girls contribute 4d. each weekly. An old woman who obtains her living by washing contributes 3d. weekly." A gentleman writing to the late Mr Ross, whose abundant labours in connection with this movement are known and appreciated in all the Churches, says, " You will feel interested in the result of your visit to us to explain the scriptural principles of weekly storing and giving, fifteen years ago. We now have a beautiful new chapel which cost £8000, with minister's house, all free from debt, with an ample weekly income. This is not the whole benefit, by the blessing of God, derived from the adoption of the principles expounded. Having charge of the church income, it was my privilege repeatedly to hear from the lips of our very dear departed Mr B—— expressions of this kind—' You don't know what a valuable means of grace I enjoy while acknowledging on a Sabbath morning the success which has attended me in business during the previous week, and gratefully laying aside the proportion due to my Redeemer's cause.'"

Institutions or customs which have come down to us from our fathers, and which are consequently associated with many of those habits which constitute a second nature, are not to be changed abruptly, even for others altogether and manifestly better. There is a preliminary process of education to which it is well to subject popular thought and feeling, in order that, the way for the reform being prepared, it may be the more quietly and thoroughly effected. We do not therefore advocate the immediate substitution of the Weekly Offering for Church Purposes for other plans, in every case, and still less the introduction of it in any instance against the wishes of a respectable minority. But we are firmly persuaded that it is in this direction that the Christian people should be looking, and that every opportunity of making an advance towards so admirable a system should be improved.

CHAPTER VIII.

PROSPERITY.

"BRING Me all the tithes into the storehouse, that there may be meat in Mine house, and prove Me now herewith, saith the Lord of Hosts, if I will not open you the windows of heaven, and pour you out a blessing, that there shall not be room enough to receive it." This passage has already been quoted, but we make no apology for reinserting it here, as no other so clearly sets forth what we are now to consider, namely, the relation between the faithful discharge by the Church of its obligations, and the enjoyment by it of material and spiritual prosperity. Such promises are not limited to those to whom they are expressly made. They are not arbitrary determinations of the Divine Will in favour of individuals, but statements of the immutable order of the Divine Government. Just as surely and as constantly as latent forces inherent in various forms of matter are evoked by every one who has discovered and fulfilled the conditions of their activity, so surely and so constantly does the blessing of God follow in the wake of magnanimous and largehearted Christian liberality. Church life is exalted, the Church becomes strong, and every member of it finds that he not only has a share in the blessedness of the general quickening, but that his own increased and more systematic acknowledgment of God's claims tend directly to the promotion of true religion in his heart. In this chapter we propose to review the advantages which would result to the Church at large. Those resulting to the individual Christian will be considered in the next.

Under such a system as we have been describing, money would flow readily, silently, and in a copious and unfailing stream into the treasury. While the temple was in course of building, we are told that there was neither hammer, nor axe, nor any tool of iron heard in the house. Quietness and unobtrusiveness in the conduct of the subsidiary work of the Church are in accordance with the instincts of devout Christians themselves, and never fail to command the approval of the wise. Such quietness and unobtrusiveness would be secured in the highest degree by the system before us. Impassioned speeches having "Give, give" as their burden, half-despairing appeals, exasperating reiterations of complaint, such as at present seem to be necessary evils, would be wholly superseded. No indirect social pressure would be brought to bear, such as so often alienates altogether the lukewarm adherents of the Church, or lowers their estimate of its worth and integrity. No unworthy approaches would be made to men of the world, in the way of asking them of their charity to spare a little for the poor Church of Christ. They would be urged to give themselves to Christ, and only asked to give of their substance to the Church 'for Jesus' sake.' The secular organization of the Church, so far from being out of harmony with its spiritual ends, would then conduce to those ends directly as well as indirectly, and even the giving and receiving of money would be blessed to many souls. How powerfully would the operation of such a system impress the world! When Christian men and women were seen giving largely to the Church, without being solicited to do so, in obedience to the promptings of their own hearts and consciences; when the rich were seen pouring out of their abundance into the treasury with unexampled profusion, and even the poorest were found contributing out of their deep poverty, and all 'for Jesus' sake,' the world would be more deeply moved than by the intimation of the largest amounts obtained by those cumbrous devices and laboriously administered systems, which are the butt of its ridicule or the occasions of its wrath, even when it submits to be persuaded into giving them its support. Many stumbling-blocks would be removed, and the Church with pristine simplicity and integrity would recover pristine strength.

But not only would the Scripture method be so much more admirable in its working than those in ordinary use, it would place a very much larger revenue at the disposal of the Church for the carrying on of its work. What has been proved in the case of the individual, would be of course found to hold equally of the society, namely, that systematic giving means increased giving. Some indeed might be found reducing their givings, on the withdrawal of the external pressure to which they yield at present. But as the duplicity and cupidity of Ananias and Sapphira stood alone, and only threw into bolder relief and made more impressive the unworldliness and unselfishness of the first Church at Jerusalem, so, such cases would be few, and would rather tend to the commendation than to the discredit of the system in connection with which they occurred. If a few, who are at present grudging givers, should under a better system give less to God than they now give to man, the loss thus sustained would be far more than counterbalanced by the vastly increased amounts, which would be forthcoming as the spontaneous offerings of those whose hearts would respond to the direct appeal to their Christian faith and love. Aid-receiving congregations would speedily become self-supporting. Congregations which at present barely raise a sufficient amount to pay the minister's stipend and to meet the working expenses, would find themselves at the close of the year with a balance in hand, which it would be their pleasant duty to allocate to the various central funds of the Church. And wealthier congregations which at present remit their hundreds to Synod Treasurers or Mission Secretaries, would be found with greater joy sending thousands.

The bearing of such increased liberality on the great and pressing work of Church Extension is very apparent. Let us take the case of a new cause originated in one of the large towns. The congregation, instead of being left to struggle on for years under a burden heavier than it can bear, meeting perhaps in a small, uncomfortable, and mean-looking room, or in an edifice sufficiently handsome, but so burdened with debt as to be a byeword to the surrounding population, would receive assistance on a liberal scale. It might even be advisable, in some cases, and under the improved system it would be possible, to pay the entire debt resting on such a Church out of the central fund, it being ascertained of course that the members themselves had done their utmost. Such a spirited policy would often be found in the end to be a prudent and successful one, even with regard to the interests of the central fund, for the energy and enthusiasm of minister and people being free for concentration on the work of building up the spiritual fabric, and no heavy debt acting as a deterrent, a congregation would in most cases be speedily formed, which would be able in its turn to contribute largely to the help of others.

The building of Churches in poor and remote districts in which they were needed, would also be undertaken, and thus an advance would be made towards the solution of the perplexing problem, How to reach the lapsed masses? Our great cities are constantly attracting large numbers from the country districts. If these persons brought with them deeply implanted religious principles, and long formed habits of church going and godly living, they would at once become members of the Christian Church in their new home, and bring to it an accession not only of numbers but also of strength. Too often, instead of this, there is an influx of an ignorant and already degraded population, from districts where church work is feebly and inefficiently prosecuted or altogether neglected; and these proceeding from bad to worse, at length throw off all restraints and sink into a state of contented vice and misery, which make them the despair of our philanthropists and even of many zealous Christian workers. The Church, by using the funds which, under a better system of giving, would be at its disposal, to establish churches, Sunday schools, and all other necessary organisations, in districts where they are needed, would do much, if not to prevent this evil, at least to meet it before it has grown too formidable and defiant. At present, very little is being done in this direction, either in town or country, compared with what needs to be done. In the Report on the General Statistics of the United Presbyterian Church, laid before the Synod in May 1875, we have this statement, "The number of congregations on the roll of the Synod in December 1873, was 615. In December 1874, the number was 616, indicating an increase of only *one* congregation during the year 1874." The universal adoption of the scriptural method of giving would at once put an end to the *laissez faire* policy which the Church has too long pursued. It would give a mighty impulse to the work of Church Extension, and the new Churches which might be planted, would repay tenfold all money and labour expended on them, in the assistance they would render in maintaining the spiritual prosperity of the Churches now existing.

But, besides facilitating the administration of judicious help from central funds to poorer Churches and districts, this better method would accumulate large sums in the hands of individuals for disposal in this way. Wealthy givers would not throw the whole of their offering into the common funds. They would wisely retain a portion, to be applied by themselves in promoting or assisting undertakings of which it might be possible for them to take some personal oversight. For the guidance of such dispensers of their own bounty, official and unprejudiced statements might be prepared, showing the exact position and also intimating the prospects of success of any new cause. To the deserving, help would thus be forthcoming immediately, and there would be no need and no excuse for resorting to the cumbrous, expensive, and objectionable methods of raising money spoken of in a previous chapter.

The Christian ministry would then be adequately supported, and would cease to be suggestive of genteel poverty and privation. A wealthy congregation would pay its minister such a stipend as would enable him to move about among his people with comfort. Justice and generosity would both be heard when pleading for greater liberality at the settlement of the amount. And in the poorest charges the minister would still be provided with a comfortable maintenance, the payments of the people being supplemented by the liberality of the richer Churches.

In this case also, the Churches themselves would be ultimately the gainers, for a larger number of talented young men, and young men of fair position, would be induced to study for the ministry, not so much by the prospect of just treatment in temporalities, as by the assurance which such improved provision would afford, that the Church was in earnest, and that it appreciated the labours of faithful ministers of Jesus Christ.

But besides the vast increase which might be expected in the efficiency of the Church as an organisation, still more desirable results would follow—namely, the quickening of its interest in its own work, the elevation of its aims, and the rendering of its motives pure and powerful. Some may feel disposed to fasten upon this statement the charge of being illogical, asserting that quickened interest, elevated aim, and pure motive are rather causes which determine systematic giving than effects produced by it. But a little reflection will show that they stand in both relations. The capitalist embarks his wealth in some particular enterprise because that enterprise appears to him to promise success, but he has no sooner identified himself with it than his interest is deepened and his approval heightened, and he becomes jealous of its reputation as commercially sound. The mother suffers much and denies herself in many ways from love to her child, but who does not know that those very sufferings and that very self-denial intensify her affection? So it is in the relations which the Christian bears to the Church. When he has acquired the habit of giving freely, systematically, and liberally to the support of the Church, for Jesus' sake, he will assuredly follow with deepened interest those movements in which he has invested the fruit of so much resolute self-control, the gifts sanctified by so many prayers. There will be a mighty increase of zeal for God's house. There will be a growing realisation of the truth that money can of itself do nothing; that it is only the minister to faith and love. The wealthy man will no longer feel, as there is reason to fear he is sometimes now made to feel, on receiving the applause of the people or the thanks of individual applicants, that having given money he has done all. The altered mode of giving will not admit of so many compliments. Where it is earnestly adopted, these will be felt to be inappropriate, and a disparagement rather than a praise of him to whom they are addressed, as implying the existence of an idea that he had done the good deed out of regard to the opinions or the wishes of men, and not for Jesus' sake. And compliments between man and man disappearing in great measure, there will be more of the ennobling and inspiring interchange of prayer and blessing between man and

God. Instead of the carelessness as to results, and the utter waste of means, which are often found in connection with our present giving, vigilance will be exercised and a wise economy of strength practised, in the spirit of the Master who "did all things well," and whose care and economy showed themselves in the memorable command to gather up the fragments that nothing might be lost. The relation between the ministers and the lay representatives of the Church would be drawn closer, and the managers or deacons to whom the care of the temporalities is entrusted, would be able, without dictating to ministers, or in any way interfering with them in the exercise of their free, independent judgment respecting their work and duty, to render most valuable help and to give excellent counsel, the result of their own practical experience, in spheres into which the minister seldom or never enters. No one can fail to see how strong a congregation thus circumstanced would be for Christian work—ministers and elders, managers and people, all working for the same ends, without cross purposes, without even purposes running on parallel lines—the secular and the spiritual—but all converging towards one point of desire. Such a congregation, like the church at Jerusalem in its palmy days, would be of one heart and of one mind. The same liberality, the same zeal, the same love would characterise it, and it might look up to heaven anticipating with confidence the same blessing of abounding success.

Another result which might be looked for would be the elevation of the moral and spiritual tone of the Church. Nothing is more important to the Church than its own integrity and purity, and there is nothing over which it is called to exercise a more jealous care. The Church is the salt of the earth, and alas for both if the salt have lost its savour! Many warnings against conformity to the world are given to us in Scripture. As we have seen, not a few of our existing means of obtaining money, if they do not actually compromise truth and holiness, lead by a way lying perilously near to the boundary line of the worldly and un-Christian. Were the Scripture method universally adopted, this source of weakness would cease to exist. Giving would then be associated with thoughts of the Great Sacrifice and Him who made it, with faith in the Unseen and the Eternal, with hopes laying hold of the rest and joy which remain after the toils and conflicts of time, and with loving wishes and prayers for the great family of man. It would no longer be the occasion of words of idle compliment or flattery on the one hand, or of equally idle words of banter on the other. It would no longer be associated with unworthy. rivalries, or be made to minister to vanity. How greatly would such changes tend to a more solemn realisation by the Church of its position and its responsibilities, and consequently to its commanding the respect even when it aroused the wrath of the world! One virtue cannot be cultivated or improved without all the others feeling the effect of the impulse. And so it would be in this case. With conscious integrity, and that noble scorn for the indirect or underhand, which the firm and consistent hold of a noble purpose gives, the Church would become rich and abound in other graces also. Simplicity and consistency, the two essential characteristics of everything truly noble in the moral and spiritual spheres, having been attained, there would grow up around them in luxuriance the benign and beautiful fruits of the Spirit.

The change would not fail to affect also most favourably the sacred office of the ministry, and to add greatly to its usefulness. "Like priest, like people," is a common adage, but the converse proposition has also its truth, for the character of a minister's services must be influenced for good or for evil by the spirit and tone prevailing among those to whom he ministers. A congregation which gives intelligently, systematically, and cheerfully to the cause of Christ has a right to expect that intelligence, careful study, and earnestness shall characterise the pulpit, and its expectation will seldom be disappointed. It is difficult to conceive of anything more depressing to an ardent and enthusiastic temperament than preaching Sabbath after Sabbath to an audience consisting of persons who are known to be alive to every other interest and active in every other sphere, but who in matters sacred, have delivered themselves over to be bound hand and foot by the bonds of old custom and routine. Too often in such cases, the minister, after ineffectual attempts to rouse his people into life and energy, himself subsides into a kindred torpor. Where there are a living interest and sustained self-denial, such a state of things cannot exist. And all over the Church, ministries at present acceptable and useful would be so reinforced and stimulated by more manifest tokens of real interest on the part of the people, as to yield fruit beyond the expectation of the most sanguine.

The relieving of ministers from the duty of superintending on many occasions the work of raising money would be an immense gain to them and to the Church. It is true, that, were systematic beneficence introduced, it would be more than ever their duty to declare to their people periodically, the whole counsel of God concerning the duty of giving, but this would be in the line of their proper function as teachers and exhorters, and it would be very different from the irksome and unbecoming tasks which they are now called upon to perform, of urging people to give to certain objects in the form of a collection to be taken at the close of the sermon. It is one thing to impress upon a congregation the Christian duty of giving to the cause of God, to adduce by way of enforcing it the authority of Scripture, and to seek to inspire with motives which will work their own perfect work in the chambers of the heart and conscience, and issue ultimately in spontaneous offerings; and it is a very different thing to urge the giving of shillings or sovereigns there and then to some particular missionary or Church fund. The former is included in the proper sphere of ministerial duty. From the latter it would be well for the Church if ministers were wholly relieved. And especially is it desirable that in those days of vexed questions, theological, moral and social, the mind of the minister should be left perfectly free to devote all its energy to the word, thought and prayer. Every day a high standard of excellence in pulpit ministrations becomes more imperative. Men are accustomed more and more to exact thinking and correct speaking; and failure to meet the requirements of educated intellect and taste entails discredit on the pulpit and on the Church. If our Churches are to hold their own in presence of popularised science and popularised literature and philosophy, it can only be by the minister's being thoroughly furnished for his work as a workman not needing to be ashamed. Where this is recognized, a system of church finance, which would enable the officebearers of Churches to relieve their ministers of all duties immediately connected with money, except the receiving of the stipend from the congregational treasurer, and the contributing of their own share of the congregational income, cannot fail highly to commend itself.

And if the ministry at home were thus reinforced in respect of numbers, ability, and permitted consecration to special work, the missionary staff would be in no less measure augmented and strengthened. A Church giving earnestly, liberally, and directly, to the support of missionary operations, would not fail to find suitable candidates for the mission field. It is the prevalent apathy of the Church respecting missionary work which affects so disastrously the supply of missionaries. Were the apathy succeeded by such interest as the Scripture system would both inspire and manifest, the difficulty would cease. If the missionaries already labouring in the foreign field, the students in our theological halls, and the children growing up in Christian families, were made to feel that this was a work dear to the heart of the Church, and knew that Sabbath after Sabbath prayers were offered, and money set aside, and many anxious wishes cherished for the success of this work, by earnest men and women; if it were plain to all that missionaries were highly esteemed for their work's sake, and that instead of the obscurity of their labours, and the detrimental effect of separation from civilized society in respect of information and culture, being allowed to discredit them, these only enhanced the respect paid to their self-denial; then the young, the enthusiastic and the brave would count it an honour to go forth to be as hands and feet to a Church inspired by views so grand, and possessing a heart so warm and true.

But if such spiritual prosperity might be expected for the Church, we do not say from the mere adoption of a new method in church finance, but from all that its adoption would imply of increased faith and love, intelligence and power, would not the Church's prosperity tell upon the world? If the Church were the arena of a vast activity, not proclaiming its own existence on the housetops, but most signally testified to by its results; if the sincerity of Christians in professing lofty aims and their determination to secure them were alike too practically manifest to be called in question; if church extension in neglected country districts and in our great cities were progressing with somewhat of that steadiness and rapidity which are characteristic of all earnest undertakings, commercial and social, in these days; if the ministry were so supported as to indicate appreciation and esteem, not only of the individuals but of the office; if the intelligent interest of the Church in its own work were everywhere apparent, and if a high moral and spiritual tone characterised its spirit; if the ministry were able, learned, enthusiastic and wholly consecrated to the high and holy work of declaring the truth as it is in Jesus; if missionary enterprises were being prosecuted with vigour, and if tidings were ever being brought of real and palpable success, how great a change would come over the relations of the Church and the World. Cynical as the World is, it always does homage ultimately to a noble simplicity and earnestness in the prosecution of worthy ends, and from respect there is but a step to companionship and imitation. Such a Church would compel from the World the acknowledgment, "Happy art thou O Israel, who is like unto thee O people saved by the Lord." And even when it was in its heart to curse, it would be constrained like Balaam to use the words of blessing, "How goodly are thy tents O Jacob, and thy tabernacles O Israel! By the valleys are they spread forth, as gardens by the river's side, as the trees of lign aloes which the Lord hath planted, and as cedar trees beside the waters!" And many a wanderer, to whom words of warning and words of entreaty had been addressed in vain, would be irresistibly moved by glimpses casually obtained of the deep faith, ardent love, and high spirit of endeavour dwelling unostentatiously in Christian hearts. Words like those of Ruth to Naomi would often cheer and delight such a Church, "Whither thou goest I will go, and where thou lodgest I will lodge; thy people shall be my people, and thy God, my God."

And if, as the sequence of an earnest living Christian Church, there should arise a truly Christian Britain, bringing its strong practical good sense, its administrative talent, its unparalleled energy, its indomitable perseverance, to bear in the promulgation of Christian truth and the diffusion of Christian holiness, then there would be good hope indeed for the world. If we have faith even as a grain of mustard seed in the divine origin and the ultimate triumph of Christianity, we shall not regard such a future as visionary. There is an accumulating power in moral and spiritual forces not less marvellous than that residing in the forces of the material world. When social movements are fairly launched, their progress often confounds the most sanguine of those by whom they were originated. And if they are in harmony with those eternal principles, conformity to which is essential to strength and continuance, there is no limit to what they may ultimately effect. Let each member of the Church but do his own duty as in the sight of God, and look carefully to the obligations he owes to God and to his fellowmen, and the obligation under which he lies to himself to be honest and consistent, and the Church will put on a new strength which will confound those of her enemies who are congratulating themselves on signs of weakness and decay, and saying, There is no help for her in God. Let the Christian Church but take up her rightful position, and then England, which has so long held a political, an intellectual, and a commercial supremacy among the nations, will acquire one nobler still, that supremacy in Christian love and labour which it is not only blessed to exercise, but which those over whom, or rather for whom, it is exercised, acknowledge without a murmur or a grudge.

Once more, let us say, we do not anticipate such things as the result of any mere change in modes of giving. But the universal adoption by the Church, of Paul's method, and faithful adherence to it, would signify a simple faith, an enduring love, an intelligent and active interest, to which all things would be possible. And not only would its adoption signify the existence of these; it would also, and this is our plea, tend to foster them. Action and reaction are constantly in progress in the Christian life. Sound principles determine right action, and a course of right action strengthens good principles. We have this truth strikingly set forth in two complementary sayings of our Lord, "If ye know these things, happy are ye if ye do them;" and "If any man will do his will, he shall know of the doctrine whether it be of God." If God points out clearly to his Church the path of duty, and she hears the voice from heaven saying, "This is the way, walk ye in it," let her not hesitate, but at once obey the heavenly vision, and as she advances in the appointed course, faith and love, hope and intelligence, will revive and receive marvellous accessions of strength, the course itself having been expressly arranged with a view to this result, by Him who perfectly understands the creatures whom He Himself has formed, and who needs not that any should testify to Him of man, seeing that He knows what is in man.

CHAPTER IX.

HIGHER CHRISTIAN LIFE.

There is one aspect of the subject which has as yet been only incidentally alluded to, and the importance of which justifies our assigning to it a special chapter. We refer to the modifying influence which the adoption of the apostolic method of giving would exert on the habits, views, and Christian life of individual members of the Church. We have seen that under the old economy temporal prosperity was promised to those who faithfully met the requirements of the law, and that this promise is still valid, having been confirmed in the New Testament. However differently we may account for it, there is as much truth now, as in the days of Solomon, in the proverb, "There is that scattereth and yet increaseth." No man is ever the poorer ultimately through adopting the practice of systematic beneficence, while we often see those who in the time of plenty have withheld more than was meet brought to poverty. But such temporal prosperity is not the blessing most prominently held forth in the promises of the Christian dispensation, which, as we have seen, is altogether more spiritual and heavenly than the Mosaic.

Every Christian ultimately receives a spiritual blessing to his own soul from that improved state of society for which he has laboured. Whatever tends to the amelioration of the conditions under which the society exists, tends necessarily to the prosperity of the individual. Between the welfare of the whole and the welfare of the part there is a necessary and constant relation. "Whether one member suffers, all the members suffer with it, or one member be honoured, all the members rejoice with it." This truth is daily forcing itself upon us in connection with sanitary law. Society in general can never enjoy perfect health, or be safe from attacks of deadly disease, while any of its members are living in violation of the elementary laws of health, and suffering in consequence. The ninety-nine may observe the conditions of cleanliness, temperance, and sufficient aeration, but if every hundredth be living in filth, or gluttony, or shut up in unventilated rooms, these latter will not only reap the fruits of their own disobedience, but will also endanger the health of their wisely and healthfully living neighbours. If the proportion of the disobedient to the obedient be inverted, and the former become the majority, the sufferings of the innocent from the results of the conduct of the guilty are greatly extended and increased. The law which thus operates in the physical realm, binding man to man by identifying the interests of each with the interest of all, prevails not less in the spheres of the moral and spiritual, though in these latter we often fail to recognise it, or to give it the consideration which it deserves. The Christian is in constant personal danger from the unbelief and the impiety of his ungodly neighbour. If he does not war against these, they will war against him, and in all probability overcome him. Thus it is that he who is not for Christ is against Him, and he who gathers not with Him, scatters. The scepticism, profanity, and degrading vice which exist only too visibly among us, and which ever and anon raise their heads so defiantly, constitute a perpetual menace to the religion of the Christian and that of his family. In such a posture of affairs, the policy of non-intervention and selfish neutrality is simply suicidal.

He who meets every solicitation to work for the good of others with the question, "Am I my brother's keeper?" is blind not only to his brother's claims but to his own interests. There is a deep significance in the solemn declaration, "When I say unto the wicked, Thou shalt surely die; and thou givest him not warning, nor speakest to warn the wicked from his wicked way, to save his life; the same wicked man shall die in his iniquity; but his blood will I require at thine hand." This recoiling of careless indifference upon itself is often observed by those who watch the course of Providence. Sins unreproved, ignorance left untaught, irreligiousness unremonstrated with, at length rise like a flood and sweep away those on whom devolved the duty, and with whom at one time rested the power, of restraining and correcting them. The Christian, in giving of his substance to build Churches, to support a Christian ministry, to promote the evangelisation of the heathen at home and abroad, to communicate religious education, to diffuse Christian literature, is in so doing "delivering his own soul," and it may be the souls of his children, and children's children. Who can tell in how many instances the reaction may be direct and speedy? The web of Providence is intricate, and we have little skill in following its design or in tracing its threads, but it is not to stretch imagination unduly to suppose a chain of causes and effects, which, beginning in the bestowal of a gift in the service of God, shall result at length in infinite spiritual blessing to the giver himself, or to some one closely related to him by ties of kindred or affection. It is well to bear in mind that this identity of the spiritual interests of the one with the spiritual interests of the many, is the appointment of God. Woe to those, then, who, self-indulgent and at ease in Zion, look out with hardened hearts upon the spectacle of a world lying in wickedness, and oppose a deaf ear to its inarticulate cry for light and healing! God is on high, and will avenge the uncared-for and the uninstructed. A day of retribution is ever imminent, and at any moment the pestilence which walks in darkness may enter the abode of the despiser and fill his soul with bitterness. Calamity at his own fireside may be the means of opening his eyes to that havoc wrought by sin, the progress of which in a thousand other homes he had viewed with unconcern. On the other hand, great is the blessedness of the man who is "watching and praying always that he may be accounted worthy to escape all those things that shall come to pass, and to stand before the Son of Man." Such an one shall in patience possess his soul, earnestly striving for the hope of the Gospel, doing good to others, seeking to love them as he loves himself, and receiving both a present and a future reward; enjoying meanwhile the blessedness of giving, and about to find, perhaps in some unlooked-for form, the bread which he now casts upon the waters returning to him after many days.

The happy influence which, through his own deeds and his own gifts, may thus ultimately be brought to bear on the Christian giver, is, although real and certain, more or less remote; but there are personal advantages directly and immediately reaped by him. Systematic giving favours the formation of many habits which are essential to a truly useful and happy life. It leads, for instance, to the substitution of simplicity for hurtful luxury in modes of living. The offering of a fair proportion of income will not allow of an unlimited expenditure for the gratification of "the lust of the flesh, the lust of the eye, and the pride of life." Our age,

K

through the abundance of its material resources, stands in great danger from these temptations. Intemperance in eating and drinking, and wasteful extravagance in dress, exist to a lamentable extent. And the evil is no longer confined to the wealthier portion of the community. It is rampant among the working classes. "Let us eat and drink, for to-morrow we die," is really the ruling maxim with tens of thousands. And the transgressors seek to shelter themselves under the cover of false theories. Ignorance and credulity become an easy prey to the apostles of a degrading sensualism. Those elementary laws of God which point to simplicity as a condition of the highest and healthiest life, are utterly ignored, in the insane rush after the enjoyment of as much idleness, as much meat and drink, as much mad excitement, as much enervating luxury as can be obtained. A luxurious age is a degenerate age, and no one who has read history with intelligence, or observed for himself the various courses of human life, can fail to be alarmed for his country, when he finds it entering on this giddy career. The self-denial involved in such giving as Scripture enjoins, and the habit of weighing the spiritual against the material, and deciding in favour of the former, are the best safeguards of the individual. How many are there who, if they were to devote to good and noble use the money which they at present expend in pampering and destroying themselves, would reap from their abstinence alone a degree of bodily health and equanimity which would amply justify the changed course of such outlay, apart altogether from the positive good effected for others, or secured for themselves!

Another result, which would be especially important to the working classes, would be the formation and encouragement of provident habits. We hold that it is the duty of many, if not of all, in a society such as ours of to-day, to make some provision against times of sickness and the period of old age. Many have been led by the practice of laying by in store on Sabbath for the service of God, to lay by a fixed sum also toward making such provision. Order, which is so conspicuous in all the works of God, is truly admirable in the life of man. And order in one department suggests and encourages the introduction of order into every other. The order instituted in connection with the noblest service in which the Christian is engaged, is almost certain to influence for good his procedure in every work to which he puts his hand. The conscientiousness exercised in the consecration of the Lord's portion will extend to the expenditure of the rest of his income, and sobriety and wisdom will preside over all monetary transactions. It is difficult to imagine one who systematically gives a fixed proportion of his income to God every Sabbath, living beyond his means, or running into debt from which he knows that he cannot extricate himself, and so involving himself in embarrassments, which are as detrimental to the growth of the Christian graces as they are destructive of peace and happiness.

The use of this method would also foster those habits of quick decision and prompt energetic action, which are so admirable in themselves, and so useful in all the engagements of life. In this particular department, which is the highest of all, the systematic giver knows what he is aiming at, why he aims at it, and what forces he has at command to secure his purpose, and thus he is ready, when the moment for action arrives, to consider how that force may be most advantageously disposed.

Besides thus beneficially affecting the habits, the adoption of this method might be expected to exercise a liberalising influence upon the mind. To have beheld the Alps, or to have trodden the streets of Rome or Jerusalem, is, even in the experience of the most ordinary natures, not merely to have been deeply moved at the time, but to have received an abiding impression of the sublimities that are hidden in God's universe, such as has enlarged both mind and heart. A power in the same direction, and greater rather than less, belongs to every vision of the Kingdom of God enjoyed by the Christian. And when a man comes to realise his own relations to that Kingdom, and to perceive with a spirit subdued by awe, that the responsibility for its advent rests upon him in common with all the faithful, he too is lifted into the domain of the sublime. "Among them that are born of women there hath not risen a greater than John the Baptist: notwithstanding he that is least in the Kingdom of Heaven is greater than he." Statesmen, financiers, and economists are accustomed to take large views of human affairs, but the sincere and consistent Christian takes a still larger view, and every day he can do something for the realisation of his great hope. It is true the sceptic tells him that the hope is so great as to be chimerical, so sublime as to pass into the region of the inane. And the professing Christian who makes no sacrifice for the Kingdom, who neither prays, nor works, nor gives to hasten its advent, virtually acquiesces in the decision of the sceptic, and acknowledges that his faith is vain. But the patient labourer for Christ, and the Christian who denies himself, so that with prayer and a loving heart he may consecrate a portion of what God has given him to secure the coming of His Kingdom, bears witness to his possession of exalted views, such as cannot be entertained without making the mind that entertains them magnanimous. The elevation of thought and the nobility of character displayed by many Christians in the humbler walks of life, have often surprised men of the world; but the co-existence of such qualities, with a sincere and practical piety, is no marvel to those who perceive the natural alliance existing between them.

The practice of systematic beneficence would be eminently serviceable in imparting that practical wisdom, which teaches us to keep in view our end and the measure of our days, and to know how frail we are. The weekly account rendered to God would remind the giver of the rapid approach of that final account to which all others point. The judicious distribution of property would suggest and greatly promote a judicious use of time. We should not then witness the humiliating spectacle of the professing Christian growing more and more attached to money, as he nears the period when, if his professed faith be well founded, he will exchange it for a treasure infinitely more precious and enduring. Every successive time of settlement would come as a glad reminder that the period of service in the lower sphere would soon be complete, and that a message might at any hour be brought, intimating, in thrilling words, the completion of service on earth and a call to enter upon it in glory.

Nathaniel Ripley Cogg was an exceptionally noble systematic giver. In November, 1821, he drew up the following document: " By the grace of God I will never be worth more than £10,000. By the grace of God I will give one fourth of the net profits of my business to charitable and religious uses. If I am ever worth £4000, I will give one half of my net profits. If I am ever worth £6000, I will give three fourths, and the whole after £10,000." He died at the early age of thirty-six, after a life of eminent usefulness and piety.

His talents and penetration had secured for him brilliant success in business, and he had faithfully kept his solemn vow. On his deathbed he gave this remarkable testimony. "Within the last few days I have had some glorious views of heaven. It is indeed a glorious thing to die. I have been active and busy in the world. I have enjoyed it as much as any one. God has prospered me. I have everything to tie me here. I am happy in my family. I have property enough. But how small and mean does the world appear when we are on a sick bed. Nothing can equal my enjoyment in the prospect of heaven. My hope in Christ is worth infinitely more than all other things." This man might have left behind him a gigantic fortune, if he had not given away amounts varying from £1000 to £3000 per annum. Was he a fool? In view of those last words, not even the most obdurate worldling would dare to pronounce him one. Wisdom is justified of such children. Even in the estimation of those who do not believe in a hereafter, a life like this must take its place side by side with that of the noble Roman who when a day had passed without his having found an opportunity to perform some act of justice to a subject, or some deed of kindness to a friend, was wont mournfully to exclaim, "I have lost a day."

Systematic Beneficence would also contribute greatly to sustain the strength and liveliness of the religious affections. The habitual doing of good and exercise of self-denial for Jesus' sake would endear the Saviour to the hearts of His people. To many, the existence of Jesus Christ is shadowy and uncertain, and that heaven, on the throne of which He is seated, dim and remote. This is due for the most part to the non-observance of those acts of fellowship and communion which Christ enjoined. And among these the performance of deeds of love in His name holds a conspicuous place. Acts are notoriously more effectual than mere words in cementing and maintaining friendships, and even He who is the chiefest among ten thousand cannot long continue to occupy a place in the hearts of those who find no other expression for their devotion than the frequent utterance of His name. We know how dearly the mother loves the sick child over whom she has watched through the weary hours of many long nights, and whom she has tended in season and out of season. We know how dearly the patriot loves the country for which he has suffered and bled. We know how the martyr in the cause of justice or truth clings the more tenaciously to the interests he has espoused, the greater the sacrifices he has had to make for them. In the same way, the sacrifices, the labours, and the loving gifts of the Christian bring him into actual communion with Christ, draw him nearer to the heart of the Saviour, and sustain his holy love in strength and ardour.

The same is true of the Christian's sympathy with his fellowmen. It too stands in need of some practical expression, otherwise it decays and is in danger of extinction. This truth has been finely set forth by a living poet,—

> " Pour forth the oil, pour boldly forth :
> It will not fail until
> Thou failest vessels to provide,
> Which it may largely fill.

> " But then, when such are found no more,—
> Though flowing broad and free
> Till then, and nourished from on high,—
> It straightway staunched will be.

> " Dig channels for the streams of Love,
>   Where they may broadly run :—
>   And Love has overflowing streams,
>   To fill them every one.
>
> " But if at any time, thou cease
>   Such channels to provide,
>   The very founts of Love for thee
>   Will soon be parched and dried.
>
> " For we must share, if we would keep,
>   That good thing from above.
>   Ceasing to give, we cease to have :—
>   Such is the Law of Love."

The sympathies of children are quickly awakened and are generally deep and tender. The spectacle of suffering, or the tale of woe, seldom fails to touch the heart and to bring a tear to the eye. But as years pass on, and experience is gained, the mind becomes habituated to the contemplation of pain and sorrow, and if the continuance of sympathy depend entirely upon the retention of the original susceptibility of the heart, it will soon cease. But when the reason and the Christian conscience are brought into exercise, and when, at their bidding, relief is frequently administered to the distressed, a wise, powerful and enduring interest in the well-being of others is formed, which is, to the susceptibility of a young heart, what the massive intellect of the man is to the quick but narrow apprehension of the child.

The necessity of a *daily* supply of divine grace to the due maintenance of the Christian life is well known to every earnest Christian. For the sustenance of the spiritual, not less than for that of the temporal life, we need to pray, "Give us *this day* our daily bread."

Faith can only be retained by a daily apprehension or recognition of the truth, and love requires for its healthful existence daily expression. It is a further recommendation of Systematic Beneficence, that, in making it possible for the Christian daily to give consideration to the claims of religion and charity, it ministers to his religious affections and enables him to preserve a tender and sympathetic heart, in spite of the hardening influences to which he is exposed.

Another of the blessings which follow in the train of this practice is the possession of a conscience void of offence towards God and man. Conscious integrity is the condition of moral courage, and the foundation of all noble character. To have known his duty and not to have done it, occasions grief to every honourable man, but when habitual acknowledgment of duty comes to be associated with habitual disregard of it, the honourable in spirit and in character is gradually undermined and destroyed. In common life this is recognised, but in respect of Christain obligations it would almost seem as if, by common consent, the expectation of strict consistency between a man's profession and his practice were waived. Yet inconsistency here is both the sign and the occasion of lamentable weakness. The systematic giver is strong in his conscious integrity. When in his prayers he acknowledges his debt to Christ, when he confesses that he is not his own, having been bought with a price, when he prays that he may be enabled to consecrate all that he has to the Master's service, when he unites with others in singing such words as these,—

> "Were the whole realm of nature mine,
> That were a present far too small;
> Love so amazing, so divine,
> Demands my soul, my life, my all,"—

he knows that he is not using, without any thought of their meaning, words which, as possessed of meaning, he could not without grim irony make his own.

We conclude with what must be a mere reference to that inestimable 'treasure in heaven,' the acquisition of which is so constantly associated by Christ with self-denial and beneficence. What is the nature of that treasure? Is it not just the share which Christ's people have, as His instruments, in bringing about that grand consummation of all things, the Kingdom of God. When that Kingdom comes and is revealed in all its magnificence and splendour, there will be simultaneously revealed both the great work of Christ as its founder and head, and all the work done by His servants at His bidding and under His direction. Not even a cup of cold water, the giving of which had contributed to the glorious issue, will be lost sight of in that day. It will then be found that on earth, no money was expended to greater advantage, none placed at higher interest, none converted into more enduring substance, than that which was bestowed, directly or indirectly, in promoting the Kingdom of God.

THE CHURCH'S EXCHEQUER.

"We can all do more than we have done
   And not be a whit the worse;
It never was loving that emptied the heart,
   Or giving that emptied the purse."

PREFATORY NOTE.

I AVAIL myself of this opportunity to express a deep feeling of thankfulness that the views expressed in the following essay have been countersigned by names so eminent as those of the adjudicators.

The following sentences from the pen of the illustrious veteran, Dr Duff, may lead some to give more attention to the subject. The letter was written in August 1875 to the Convener of the Free Church of Scotland's Committee on Systematic Giving.

"The object is one not of secondary but of primary importance. But for ages it has been so neglected that much time and labour, and faith and patience, with the accompanying blessing of God's Holy Spirit, will be needed to work it into the mind and heart of the Church at large.

"The spirit of the age, in its rampant secularity and luxuriousness, is sadly against it. But that is no reason, but the contrary, for not strenuously persevering in the good work.

"If Revivalism is to end merely in a spiritual luxuriousness and self-complacency and self-enjoyment—though of a decidedly higher kind than the worldly and the carnal—it will only prove a more refined kind of selfishness, the very opposite of the out-going spirit—the Divinely exemplified spirit—of self-denying love.

"Ah! if there were more of this Divine Spirit amongst us, soon would the object of your Committee find a development and enlargement that would speedily fill the whole earth with its blessed fruits.

"Meanwhile, let faith, with perseverance and prayer, be the motto. Yours very sincerely, ALEXANDER DUFF."

In the spirit of these valuable words, I would venture to press on those who may become interested in this great subject the importance of frequent conferences for the exposition and discussion of it in its practical bearings. While publications such as the present are fitted to be very useful, it is to the living voice we must look for carrying Scriptural principles to every corner of the Church, and for securing their permanent influence.   A. M. S.

CONTENTS.

	PAGE
Introduction	159

CHAPTER I.—FUNDAMENTAL PRINCIPLES.

I. The genius of Christianity requires that all our Giving be *Voluntary*, *Hearty*, and *Conscientious*	161
II. *Careful Preparation for Giving is Scriptural* and *Necessary*	165
III. *Giving is the Duty and Privilege of every believer*	170

CHAPTER II.—THE CHURCH'S EXCHEQUER.

The Bible method stated 173
The Bible method proved by arguments—
  I. We are to give *first to God* 174
  II. The teaching of Scripture *concerning Tithes*—
    1. The tithe *is not Jewish* 176
    2. The *Principle* of the tithe 178
    3. *Abraham's* tithes (Heb. vii. 4) 179
    4. *Jacob's* tithes (Genesis xxviii. 11-22) . . 180
    5. *Meaning* of Mal. iii. 10 182
    6. How far all this guides us in regard to *the amount we should give* 183
  III. *Our Relation to the Lord Jesus Christ in the matter of Giving*—
    1. His *Example* 186
    2. His *Eye* 187
    3. His *Glory in Heaven* 192
    4. His *Love* 193
  IV. *The New Testament Rule in* 1 Cor. xvi. 1, 2—Defence of its *authority for us* 195
    1. It supplies each man with a rule for calculating the portion *he* is to give 199
    2. It requires us to consider our giving to God *once a week* 202
    3. "On the *First Day* of the week" . . . 205
    4. "Everyone by himself" 208
    5. Θησαυρίζων. Treasure in heaven . . . 209
    6. The Rule is *universal* 210

CHAPTER III.—The Church's Exchequer pleaded for on the Ground of its Advantages.

PAGE

I. *Advantages* to the Individual—
  1. He will always have something to give and will give it pleasantly 212
  2. He is protected from unpleasant solicitation . . . 216
  3. It promotes his *temporal* prosperity—
    (Mr Gladstone's opinion) 217
    The blessing of God 217
    Cases 218
  4. It promotes his *spiritual* prosperity—
    § 1. Humility 221
    § 2. Treasure in heaven 222
    § 3. Escape from the church-member's sin . . 224
      Andrew Fuller's warning 226

II. Advantages *to the Church—*
  1. *Happy Change in gathering Funds,* . . . 228
    Collecting 229
    Pew-rents 229
    "No gatherings when *I* come" 230
    Fancy-fairs 231
  2. *Increases the amount given—*
    § 1. No wet days 232
    § 2. Frequency 233
    § 3. Proportion and the growth of incomes . . 234
    § 4. Freeness : Gift v. Payment . . . 235
  3. *Benefits the poorer members—*
    § 1. Reduces their number 236
    2. Increases the number of helpers . . 237
    § 3. Help is better applied 237
  4. *Brings blessing on what is given—*
    Reasonable to expect this 237
    Humility and Prayer 238

CHAPTER IV.—Objections.

I. '*You propose a Revolution*' 240
II. '*We cannot ascertain how we stand every week*' . 240
III. '*Taxation! We like to give from free impulse*' . 242
IV. '*Let not thy left hand know what thy right hand doeth*' . 243

Conclusion, ... 243

INTRODUCTION.

IN this plea the Christian conscience and the Christian heart will be taken into account all through.

Long ago, at the close of a meeting, a worthy magistrate in Scotland said to one who had been giving an explanation of the principles of systematic Christian finance, "Your plan is excellent, Sir; but surely you go too far in taking for granted that *everybody has a conscience!*"

On another occasion, in England, the same advocate was asked by his host, a shrewd and successful merchant, to explain what it was he had come to lecture about. The explanation was given with some enthusiasm, and the merchant said, with an odd smile, half amusement, half pity, "My good friend, it is a very fine plan; but you are going in the teeth of human nature."

So we are. But we are safe in assuming that every man has a conscience, however inactive it may sometimes be; and, in pleading with those who profess to have been redeemed with the precious blood of Christ, we have a right to appeal to principles that press hard on our old man.

This plea is not intended to deal with the whole subject of Christian giving, nor will it, directly at least, urge the giving of larger amounts. In Great Britain a large amount of money is expended in maintaining the ordinances of religion among ourselves, and a large amount is bestowed in charity, and a large amount is applied toward the diffusion of the Gospel in other lands; that is to say, these amounts, presented by themselves, seem very large. But amount is always relative.* The question has to be asked—a question which the story of the widow's two mites will not suffer us to blink—Do these large sums bear a satisfactory proportion to our wealth? Referring to the Lancashire Famine Fund, Mr Gladstone said: "A country with an aggregate income in the three kingdoms of between five and six hundred millions a year, with an income subject to income-tax of between two and three hundred millions a year, ought not to think much of raising a million or two by subscription to meet a great and extraordinary distress." † Yet the annual income of all our great Bible and missionary societies together falls under one million.

But amount is not the only nor the chief consideration. Great improvement is needed in the methods of raising funds. Operose and expensive machinery, speeches, sermons, collectors going from house to house, secretaries going from town to town,—the clamant wants of men's bodies and souls, excuse the use of such means; at the same time many, weary and ashamed, are asking whether no more simple and less questionable methods can be found. Our aim is to supply an

---

* "Quia non quantum detur sed quantum resideat expenditur."
Ambrose on Mark xii. 43.

† This was in 1862. Being asked what correction he would be disposed to make in this estimate in 1876, Mr Gladstone has very courteously replied thus: "I think 500 to 600 millions was low even at the time. I should certainly now say 800 to 900 millions: and the portion of it subject to income-tax nearer 400 millions than 300 millions. I was then, however, in a condition to examine the matter minutely and speak confidently. I have now only general information, and require a wider margin."

6

answer by expounding and urging the scriptural principles by which all giving in the name of the Lord Jesus Christ ought to be regulated. Here lies the root of the matter: let men's minds be informed and their hearts persuaded concerning these principles, and not only will the amount given be what it ought to be, but the manner of giving will be simple and pleasant, and the spirit accompanying the giving will be such as to bring down upon our ecclesiastical finances that blessing which is always urgently needed, but too often never thought of. For the wider and more earnest recognition of these principles we plead. The teachings of the Word regarding the relation in which our use of money stands to the glory of Christ and to our own spiritual welfare are more full and explicit than many think; and the chief hope of permanent improvement in all that concerns the Church's Exchequer lies in getting the individual mind better informed about these teachings and the individual conscience and heart quickened into thorough and obedient reception of them. For every man *has* a conscience, and every Christian *has* a new heart.

CHAPTER I.

FUNDAMENTAL PRINCIPLES.

THESE are three. And let them not be hastily passed over as too obvious and familiar to need to be urged.

I. *The genius of Christianity requires that all our giving be voluntary, hearty and conscientious.*

What we wish to express is this: the believer best carries out the spirit of his faith when he gives rather in compliance with the dictates of an enlightened conscience and the promptings of a warm heart than in obedience to any formal or informal assessment by his fellowmen. And thus far, all who have been actively engaged in the work of Christ will go with us, even although they be members of an established church.

It is not only the adherents of an establishment who are in danger of losing sight of this first principle. Custom, habit, the use and wont of generations, have imposed something unpleasantly like assessment on the members of churches that have no connection with the State and no favour for the establishment idea. Well-meaning persons, with more zeal than enlightenment, when asking their neighbours for money sometimes urge too exclusively such motives as, what others are giving —what income the person solicited has or is supposed to have—what he ought to give, in the judgment of the person soliciting—and the like; and in every instance in which this sort of dealing by his fellowman has the chief influence on the giver's mind, it does amount virtually to an assessment. Here comes in also the influence of subscription books "well headed," as the phrase is, and of printed lists; also the difficult question of pew rents. Without turning aside to the discussion of these just now, let it be said that taxation may be enforced by social and congregational opinion almost as effectively as by civil law: and the evil then is that the giving is regulated too much by a human and too little by a divine standard, that the giver has too much regard to his estimation in the eyes of those about him, while his conscience and heart are too little exercised toward the Lord Jesus Christ. These considerations

FUNDAMENTAL PRINCIPLES. 163

cannot be, ought not to be, altogether excluded; but where they chiefly influence the giver giving is not perfectly voluntary, is not a pure outcome of the free, hearty Christian will. "Every man, *according as he purposeth in his heart*, so let him give; not grudgingly, or of necessity: for God loveth a cheerful giver." (2 Cor. ix. 7.) This is the New Testament principle, and the only satisfactory one. "I speak not by commandment, but by occasion of the forwardness of others, and *to prove the sincerity of your love*." (2 Cor. viii. 8.) Paul does not mean that what he wrote was without the authority of the Holy Spirit; but the Spirit of Christ moves him to tell the Corinthians that their giving must not rest upon mere submission to his authority; with that, another and higher principle must come into play. "For ye know the grace of our Lord Jesus Christ, that, though He was rich, yet for your sakes He became poor, that ye through His poverty might be rich." These are the next words, and they raise the whole matter of asking and giving money for Christian purposes into a region above that in which assessment of any kind finds place. Submission to the will of God expressed in His word will certainly influence our giving, but love also must come in to clothe and beautify the naked form of obedience.

This principle belongs to the Old Testament as well as to the New. As for alms-giving, its teaching was: "The poor shall never cease out of the land; therefore I command thee, saying, Thou shalt open thy hand wide unto thy brother, to thy poor, and to thy needy, in thy land" (Deut. xv. 11); and Paul (2 Cor. ix. 9, 10), cannot go beyond, but takes up and endorses, the language of the 112th Psalm on this matter. As to the support of public worship, it should be remembered that both the tabernacle and the temple were erected by offerings entirely voluntary and hearty. "Take ye from among you an offering unto the Lord; *whosoever is of a willing heart, let him bring it,* an offering of the Lord: gold, and silver, and brass," etc. "And they came, every one whose heart stirred him up, and everyone whom his spirit made willing." (Exodus xxxv. 5, 21.) The result of this appeal, not to fear but to love, was that the superintendents of the work had to tell Moses, "The people bring much more than enough for the service of the work, which the Lord commanded to make:" and a proclamation had to be issued by which "the people were restrained from bringing." (Exodus xxxvi. 4-6.) We do not know any modern instance of this kind. When the materials for the temple were prepared it was in the same manner. David gave the example of a freewill offering, "because," said he, "I have set my affection to the house of my God;" and then made the appeal, "who is willing to consecrate his service this day unto the Lord?" "Then the people rejoiced, for that they offered willingly, because that *with perfect heart they offered willingly to the Lord.*" (1 Chron. xxix. 1-19.) In the soul-stirring thanksgiving the king poured out to Him "from whom both riches and honour come," the same feature is mentioned often and with emphasis.

Such passages as these make it very clear that while Judaism, agreeably to its purposely burdensome spirit, had certain definite enforced taxations, the spiritual life of the Jewish church rose, and was taught to rise, above such temporary limitations into the atmosphere of heart-moved gratitude, of loving freeness. The Christian dispensation knows no other spirit.

Before advancing farther, let this first principle be pressed. It is not for the glory of God, it is not for the good of the church or of the Christian giver, that any minister, elder, deacon, collector, any church-court or benevolent society, should come between God and the conscience in this matter of giving. What is true in respect of all preaching and religious forms is emphatically true in this case. Turn to the first page of the history of the Christian Church. Luke, after his manner, first states in general terms how the wants of the infant church were met, and then gives two examples, the one very good, the other very bad. Barnabas "the good man"* gave rightly because out of zeal for Christ and self-denying love for his brethren; Ananias and Sapphira gave wrongly, because the regard they ought to have had towards the Searcher of hearts was deceitfully supplanted by regard to man's esteem. Why was their sin so awfully detected and avenged, if not to teach us that it is a sin specially hateful in the eye of God? Yet who will venture to say that all our ordinary givings are acceptable to Him who still "sits over against His treasury and scrutinizes" not what the people cast in, but "*how?*" (ἐθεώρει, Mark xii. 41.)

II. *Careful preparation for giving is Scriptural and necessary.*

Some who might heartily agree with our first principle may think this second one rather at variance with it. They imagine care, thought, method, must interfere with free-will: but such a notion comes only of hasty thinking or no thinking at all, and is disproved by experience. If Christian free-will were the same with the impulse of emotion created by the sight of suffering or by pathetic

---

* It is worth noting that only two persons have the honour to be called "good" in the New Testament—this Barnabas (Acts xi. 24), and Joseph of Arimathea (Luke xxiii. 50), both men of large-handed and large-hearted beneficence.

appeal, the too common opinion would be right; but Christian free-will cannot be carefully enough distinguished from such momentary impulses. An impulse and a principle are very different things; the impulse is good so far as it goes, but it is uncertain, brief, and, unless the principle lie behind it, ineffective. Witness the Levite whose impulse led him to cross the road and look at the half-murdered man, in contrast with the Samaritan who " had compassion " (Luke x. 25-37), a principle working with the quiet force of a law of nature and securing that his well-doing should be considerate, delicate, thorough, extending to the next day and beyond.

We plead that in this great matter, after the heart is roused to feel the power of Christian motives constraining to give, there shall come in careful consideration of the amount to be given and steady use of the best method. Something is to be said further on about the amount and the method; but meanwhile it is the general rule or principle that is urged.

Think. If Christians do not apply to their giving the same thought they apply to worldly affairs, they cannot know with decent accuracy what amount is at their disposal to give; and they will give either too much or too little. In most cases persons—and many of these by no means covetous or hard-hearted—will err on the side of giving far less than they would have found themselves able to give had they taken time to consider and plan: but if some err on the other side and give too much, will their conduct be more pleasing to God? The man whose heart prompts him to consider how much he can give, to pray over it, and to have it ready before the call comes, puts more honour on the Divine will and the Divine love than the man who scarcely thinks of giving except when a particular claim is presented, and then throws from him what he can easily spare, or possibly what he ought to have used in another way.

The argument from Scripture as to this principle is more full and affecting than many think. The consideration and method pleaded for are implied in all that is said regarding *the Tithe*. Presently we must say something about the relation in which the tithe stands to the Christian dispensation: it is only mentioned here to fix attention on the fact that thought and method are obviously implied in it. If it should be said that under the Mosaic economy public regulations took the consideration of the tithe out of the hands of the individual giver, we answer, that could not be said of the tithes given by Abraham and by Jacob, neither can it apply to that much-abused text Mal. iii. 10.

"Let him that stole steal no more; but rather let him labour, working with his hands the thing which is good, *that he may have to give to him that needeth*" (Eph. iv. 28), is a significant text. The first time the converted thieves in Ephesus went to church after Paul's letter came, they would be taught, not only that Christianity required them to work for their own support, but also that while working they were to think that part of their honest earnings should be held in readiness for the relief of such cases of want as they came into contact with.

There is one passage more fruitful in teaching as to Christian giving than almost any other, a passage to which we shall return more than once, John xiii. 29. Here we have the gracious example of our Lord Jesus Christ:—"Then said Jesus unto Judas, That thou doest do quickly. Now no man at the table knew for what intent He said this unto him. For some of them thought because Judas had the bag that Jesus had said unto him, Buy those things that we have need of against the feast; or, That he should give something to the poor." Like men, the faithful eleven could not refrain from guessing at their Master's meaning, and one of themselves tells us what the guesses were. There was no occasion to "buy meat" (the only use of the contents of the Bag before mentioned, John iv. 8), and there were just two other uses which the known habits of the Lord Jesus allowed them to think probable—the support of ordinances, and the relief of the poor. "Here is the primitive form of a church fund." * This example, even more than that of the converted thief in Ephesus or that of Paul (Gal. ii. 10), covers the entire breadth of the Church's membership; for we know how scantily that bag was furnished. Why did that bag exist under the control of Jesus of Nazareth if not that in the matter of the honest and pious use of money He might "leave us an example that we should follow His steps?" And to what does the example amount? Ponder again the three uses:—

1. "*To buy meat*,"—providing honestly for daily wants;

2. "*To provide things needed for the feast*,"—God's ordinances;

3. To "*give something to the poor*,"—charity.

Now the point to be marked especially is that, unless Jesus of Nazareth had been *in the habit* of thus giving, unless He had *always stood prepared to give* spontaneously and promptly, the disciples could not have guessed as they did. *He* did not wait till a Levite or a deacon came soliciting something toward keeping up the public worship of God: *He* did not say, Time enough

* Dr Christopher Wordsworth *in loco*.

to think of giving to the poor when their spirit has been crushed out by misery and they stand whining at your door. He gave spontaneously, because He was, by forethought, habit, and method, ALWAYS PREPARED FOR GIVING. We urge this as a fundamental principle, inculcated by what is far better than the plainest precept, the supreme example of Him who "for our sakes became poor that we through His poverty might be rich."

Yet if any crave more explicit teaching we have it, and given by the Holy Spirit under very instructive circumstances. "So labouring ye ought to support the weak, and *to remember the words of the Lord Jesus, how He said, It is more blessed to give than to receive.*" (Acts xx. 35.) Some may read these pages who have never considered, or had explained to them, the remarkable points of instruction about this saying. Let them think, How did Paul get hold of the saying? He had never seen the Lord Jesus on earth: he had found the saying floating among the Christian communities as a maxim of the first authority. In what circumstances does he repeat it? As a last emphatic lesson to those who were to "feed the flock of God" in the churches of Asia Minor, of which Ephesus was the centre. Whenever and wherever these men should, all their lives, discharge the office laid on them of feeding souls with the truth as it is in Christ Jesus, they would remember *this* part of the truth and urge it. How has the saying come to us? It is not found in any of the four Gospels: left a little longer to the keeping of oral tradition its purity would have been corrupted and its supreme authority weakened: but the Holy Spirit snatches it from such a fate, and, by the lips of Paul and the pen of Luke, secures for it a place of more manifest authority, and of more powerful influence upon the believer's heart to all generations. And (to bring all this to bearing on the principle for which we are pleading), How could Paul or any of the elders of Ephesus or those taught by them, how can we, secure this greater blessedness of the giver if not by consideration and method beforehand so as to stand always prepared for giving?

III. *To give for the glory and service of Christ is the duty and privilege of every believer.*

This is the only other principle that we need to insist on before more directly expounding the teaching of Scripture as to the amount and method of our givings.

There is a tendency to think that giving cannot be the duty of *every* Christian without exception, that poverty —but who shall define the degree of poverty?—must exempt from the duty and exclude from the privilege. But this cannot be.

Reflect on the nature of the case. What are the *springs* from which Christian giving flows? They are gratitude to God, love to God and man: but obviously we dare not draw a line and say, All whose income comes up to this mark *may* allow their conduct to be affected by this motive, but all whose income falls under it may not; if the impulse to give rises warm in their hearts they must crush it. Again, reflect on the *benefits* which the exercise of this grace brings to the giver: it maintains his sense of dependence on God; it keeps the love of this world in check; it strengthens the best feelings of our hearts; it fills them with the purest joy. Is there any degree of poverty that is to exclude a Christian from these? Think of the startlingly direct relation in which this whole matter stands to final judgment: "A cup of cold water shall not lose its reward;" "inasmuch as ye did it unto the least of these my brethren, ye did it unto me." We see how false the notion must be when it would have the effect of placing some on the left hand on no other ground but poverty.

Think of the tenor of Scripture in relation to this principle. The texts just brought forward with another purpose are plain enough. If the man who has but newly begun to earn his bread by honest toil is to give, who is not to give? If He gave who said, "Foxes have holes and the birds of the air have nests, but the Son of Man hath not where to lay His head" (Luke ix. 58), who is excluded from the privilege of imitating Him? In that day when the widow's two mites are brought forth and restored to her with heavenly interest, it will be felt that God has excluded no one from laying up treasure in a "bag which waxeth not old."

We must return to this subject when we come to the "*every one of you*" in 1 Cor. xvi. 2. Enough has been said to show that the duty and privilege of Giving must be strictly universal among the members of Christ's body. It is nothing but the wretched habit of looking to the *quantity* and forgetting the *quality*, of thinking only of the amount given and scarcely at all of the spirit in which the gift is offered, that creates difficulty in understanding this principle. Those who regard agricultural labourers, domestic servants, sempstresses, persons in reduced circumstances, or even those who receive charity, as too poor to give anything, do them a very questionable kindness in respect of either their spiritual or their temporal well-being. Besides, the more narrowly you watch the lives of the godly poor, you will find it a mistake to suppose they do *not* give, and often and largely too, after the widow's measure. The late Mrs Graham (whose life, entitled "the Power of Faith," was a favourite book with pious women of the last generation), for a time supported herself, her father, and four children by keeping a small school in Paisley. While enjoying comparative affluence as an officer's wife, this lady had formed the habit of setting apart a definite proportion of her income for God, and when now sorely reduced, " her dinner, potatoes and salt, her breakfast and supper, porridge," she steadfastly kept up her habit. She deducted the Lord's portion from each small sum as it came into her hands before allowing that sum to mingle with what she regarded as her own income; and thus, so long as she had "bread to eat and raiment to put on," she had always something to give, and as good a conscience and as full blessing in giving, it as in her days of plenty. The present writer went once to the house of a widow who supported herself and her mother by toiling day and night at a coarse and covetously ill-paid kind of needlework, with the purpose of finding out how she might be helped. As soon as she got a glimpse of his errand, the widow rose and produced from a corner half-a-crown, asking him to get it applied for Jewish missions. That was many years ago; and, though never administered by the hand of human charity, the widow's "bread has been given her, and her water has been sure." *

If any reader is perplexed to understand how such cases can be, let him look out a case for himself.

* While it is necessary to expound the principle as being thus universal, we must not be misunderstood. It is right to declare what the Bible teaches to rich and poor alike, and then to leave the truth to be applied by each man to himself; but the cases are few in which it is either right or wise to tell a man that he ought to give so much or anything at all. We may not pronounce any class too poor to give; but we may feel that many are too poor to be asked to give.

CHAPTER II.

THE CHURCH'S EXCHEQUER.

We shall assume that those with whom we plead admit that the heart and conscience of each member of Christ's body ought to be exercised about giving: that the most hearty free-will is not at all inconsistent with forethought and method, but will rather prompt to these in order that our giving may be ready and effective: and that these principles are universal in their application.

How are they to be applied? Does the Word of God yield us further instruction and indicate THE METHOD by which the Christian may regulate his giving so as to promote the glory of God most fully, and to secure for himself in the largest measure the benefits that flow from serving God in this matter? We believe that it does.

1. A definite proportion of income should be consecrated to God, to be spent in religion and charity.
2. This proportion should be considered and set apart once a week.
3. And, on the first day of the week.
4. The only responsible administrator of this fund is the believer himself. It is given first to God: the giving to any public fund, or to the needy, comes after.
5. This is to be made a matter of steadfast habit.

Such a habit being formed generally by the people of Christ, the Church of Christ on earth will have an Exchequer always full, being steadily supplied by the spontaneous action of conscience under the guidance of Scriptural principle and method.

We might—and further on we will—plead for this method on the ground of the benefits resulting from it, and on the ground of experience. First, however, we must ask you to consider carefully the teaching of Scripture concerning the matter. Unless this be understood and accepted there is not much hope of extensive or permanent improvement in our Christian finance. Indolence must be stirred up, the heart must be thoroughly engaged, old and cold and unblessed routine must be supplanted by fresh, warm, intelligent, and gracious habit.

I. It will be admitted by all that *we are taught in His Word* TO GIVE TO GOD. We wish this to be thought about and felt as well as admitted. How many give in the merest routine! how many never think of giving till a fellowman asks them, and yet delude themselves with a fancy that they are somehow giving to God!*

"Render *unto God* the things which are God's," is the rule laid down by our Lord and illustrated by His example. And He intended His hearers to feel that certainly not less integrity and regularity should come into play in doing this than in "rendering unto Cæsar the things that are his." (Matt. xxii. 21.) The idea is one which the common mind can well enough understand, and does understand. The money is spent in keeping up the ordinances of religion at home, in missions to Jews and Gentiles, in showing mercy to the

---

* A certain Fifeshire laird discovered after reaching his pew one Sabbath morning that he had put a crown-piece into the plate, and had thus given four shillings and elevenpence too much. The service not having begun, he rose and explained the sad mistake to the elder at the door, offering his penny and asking back his crown. But the elder told him it was very wrong to think of grudging what had been given at the Church door, and refused. The laird went away grumbling, "Weel, I suppose I'll get credit for it somewhere else." "Na, na," said the elder, "*there* ye'll get credit only for the penny."

poor; but everybody can easily apprehend the practical idea that *before* being spent in any of these ways the money is first consecrated to Him who seeth in secret. It is certainly not a new idea. It is as old as Jacob,— "I will surely give the tenth *unto Thee*" (Gen. xxviii. 22); as old as David, "Of Thine own have we given *Thee*" (1 Chron. xxix. 14); as old as Solomon, "Honour *the Lord* with thy substance" (Prov. iii. 9): and its age is greatly in its favour. But it needs to be constantly insisted on.

Indeed this is the only argument for giving which can absolutely command the heart. "*The Lord hath need*" (Luke xix. 31-34) is a startling text. How can it be true? The earth is His and the fulness thereof: "If I were hungry I would not tell thee." (Ps. l. 12.) The Maker and Sustainer of all things cannot in the ordinary sense of the word have need of us or our money. Notwithstanding, there is a sense, and that a very real and intelligible one, in which He has urgent need of our time and our property. He who gives us each day our daily bread, and blesses our industry, and casts around our substance the shield of His commandment, has been pleased to create this necessity and so to frame the constitution of this world and the dispensation of the Gospel as that there shall be real giving on our part and receiving on His. There was at that moment a need that the prophecy given centuries ago by Zechariah should be fulfilled, and the same Lord whose proper Godhead that prophecy demonstrated, was present in the person of Jesus of Nazareth needing that the animals mentioned in the prediction should be given to Him by a willing and obedient heart. It is inexhaustibly wonderful, it is amazingly gracious; but it is quite an obvious truth. At this moment the same

Lord has a larger and more urgent need: He needs our time and labour and money that He may have a visible house on earth, that the travail of His soul may be gathered in from all parts of the earth, that the poor whom He has bequeathed to us as the abiding remembrancers of His humiliation may be succoured. (Mark xiv. 7.) Remembering how much we owe to God our Saviour, and feeling that this great and real need has been graciously created by Him who has all the resources of the universe, material and spiritual, at His command, in order to link us and our perishing substance with His work of grace on earth and His eternal glory in heaven, we will devote our money *to Him first,* and so stand prepared to apply it so soon as, with reference to any particular case, the inward whisper is heard, "The Lord hath need."

It was thus that St Francis foiled Satan, and if we form the habit of frequently and sincerely devoting part of our income to God, we will not lose our reward even in those cases in which we may discover that a mistaken use has been made of the money so devoted. One day (if the legend be true, and it ought to be), a very poor monk craved charity from St Francis, and got it.

"Ha! ha!" said Satan, throwing off the beggar's rags, "You, holy man, have given alms to the devil!"

"Not so," said the saint, "I had given the money to God before I saw you or you saw me. He is not mocked: therefore I am not deceived." (Gal. vi. 7.)

II. *At this stage of our argument we crave attention to* THE TEACHING OF SCRIPTURE CONCERNING TITHES.

1. It is necessary (though it should not be necessary), to begin by setting out of the way a common prejudice to the effect that the Tithe is a Jewish thing, now of

course abolished. Those who talk thus are strangely ignorant of their Bibles. The Tithe is no more a Jewish thing than the church membership of infants and the Lord's Day are Jewish things. It is quite true that the whole cumbrous and purposely burdensome system ordained under Moses is abolished: but the Tithe had existed under the dispensation of Promise at least four hundred and thirty years before that law, which was never intended to be of universal and permanent obligation, came into existence at Sinai. Read carefully the third chapter of the Epistle to the Galatians. You will there find in a compact and plain form the substance of New Testament teaching concerning the system of rites, including tithes, which is properly called Judaism, and concerning the relation in which the Gospel, when it had abolished Judaism, remained to the primeval Promise which it did not abolish. The Covenant confirmed before of God to Abraham,—the covenant which secures acceptance and grace to all who are the children of Abraham in virtue of exercising the same simple faith in God's promise,—had a distinct reference to Christ; and so far from that covenant being abolished, it was fully perfected and established by Christ. The difference between Abraham and us is only this,—while "*Abraham* saw the day of Christ only afar off," " Jesus Christ has been evidently set forth, crucified in the midst of *us.*" " If we are Christ's we are Abraham's seed and heirs according to the Promise;" and the lesson for us touching this matter of giving is put with emphasis by our Master, " If ye were Abraham's children ye would do the works of Abraham." (John viii. 39.) Granted freely that all the minute taxation of the Mosaic economy came to an end together with the temple, yet the works of

Abraham remain an authoritative example for us, just as his faith does.*

2. A word on *the Principle* of the Tithe will prepare us for considering the patriarchal tithe-giving. What that is has been admirably stated by Mr Arthur in his famous lecture on proportionate giving. "When an arbitrary proportion of our time or goods is taken—a proportion for which reason has no more to say than for any other—what is the effect upon the mind? It serves as a practical claim of sovereignty on the part of the Creator. It says, 'This is claimed, because all might be claimed. He who accepts this, owns all, and holds you to account for the rest.' It is not probable that, year after year, one will carefully set apart a fixed proportion for the service of God, without becoming habituated to feel that he is neither author nor owner of any fraction of property, but merely steward; and that He at whose feet he lays the first-fruits is the Lord, the Giver of all." † Think over this. It is scarcely time yet to discuss the question whether a tenth is the amount which every Christian should consecrate; but, such being the essential principle of the Tithe, we cannot refuse the inference that it is a principle of universal and permanent obligation. The Gospel has taken away no privilege enjoyed before by the people of God. The exact proportion given may not be a tenth; it may be left to each to fix his own proportion: but seeing it was

---

* 1. The Law (Judaism proper), was a "schoolmaster," a child-leader (παιδαγωγὸς), "to bring us to Christ," and therefore severe. As soon as it had served its purpose it passed away.

2. The promise of God existed long before, and the Law, coming in after, "could not disannul" "the covenant confirmed before of God." (v. 17.)

3. Abraham is the father of *all* them that believe, without respect to nation (vv. 28, 29; see also Rom. iv.)

† Arthur's Lecture, pp. 35, 36.

a privilege, enjoyed long before Judaism existed, to maintain the sense of dependence on God for everything by a fixed and habitual giving of a definite proportion to Him, we cannot imagine this privilege to have ceased altogether. Human nature is the same in all generations, and God deals with it always on the same essential principles: there has been no change in the doctrine of justification by faith in atoning blood since the days of Abel, neither has there been any change in the essential use of giving, at least since the days of Abraham.

3. I say "at least," for the manner in which Abraham's tithe-giving is mentioned both in the Old Testament and in the New (Gen. xiv. 20; Heb. vii. 4), suggests that the practice did not then suddenly originate. It was when he was coming home laden with the spoils of war that the patriarch was met by the priest of the Most High God and gave to him these tithes. It is not hinted that the priest told Abraham how much he was to give, or that he was to give anything at all: one naturally thinks, therefore, that he must have known the proportion and practised the giving of it before. However that may be, we are carried back by this instance to the ruddy east, to the pure glad dawn of Grace over a dark world.

Ponder *to whom* these tithes were given. In the book of Genesis Melchizedec starts up suddenly before us, a great and mysterious personage, greater than the hero of faith, and gracious withal. The hundred and tenth Psalm gives us some light concerning him; and the Epistle to the Hebrews makes the light full. He was a "king" as well as a priest: he was the king "of Righteousness," and the king "of Peace:" he lived many centuries before the Aaronic priesthood was instituted: and whereas their office was regulated by an exact genealogy in which account was taken of both father and mother, his was under no such limitation. All this, we are told, was expressly arranged with the purpose of making him "like unto the Son of God"—the only type of His Person and of the singleness of His priesthood. Therefore, in the very same sense in which our Lord says that Abraham "saw His day and was glad," it may be said that Abraham gave tithes to the Lord Jesus Christ. This is Paul's argument. The giving of tithes was a grateful recognition by "him that had the promises" of One who had the power to bless him, "and without all contradiction the less is blessed of the better." (Heb. vii. 7, 8.) The transaction was not a lifeless form gone through between two dying men, but had express regard to the spiritual and eternal realities; for of Him who received Abraham's tithes "it is witnessed *that he liveth.*"* We are thus very directly led to connect the giving of a proportion of our property with thoughts of our great High Priest, to feel that in the truest sense it is given to Him who is our king of Righteousness and of Peace, "who sits a Priest upon His throne" (Zech. vi. 13), interceding for us and imparting to our offerings all their fragrance and acceptance.

4. The case of Abraham's grandson is much to our purpose. (Gen. xxviii. 20-22.) You cannot well think of circumstances farther removed from taxation or assessment of any kind than those in which Jacob made his vow. It was the crisis of his life: God found him in the solitude of night, a convicted sinner, alone, a fugitive: God revealed Himself to him in all His majesty and grace, shewing an open and trodden way between the sinner and Himself—scarcely to Nathanael was a fuller

---

* Compare—"*He shall live,* and to Him shall be given the gold of Sheba."—Ps. lxxii. 15.

revelation given (John i. 51): God gave to him the heritage of Abraham and Isaac in promise, and pledged his providential care. The response of Jacob consisted in an act of adoring worship (vv. 16-18), and in a solemn engagement to devote thenceforth to God, as his God, a tenth of all that he should receive from Him. The "if" is not (as has been hastily suggested) *dubitative*, as though the bargaining disposition of the patriarch was even here intruding itself; but reduplicates upon God's promises in verse 15th, and expresses, according to Hebrew idiom, certainty in the strongest form.* The points of instruction for us in this case are :—

(1) That the sinner and God were face to face under circumstances most searching and gracious to the sinner's soul.

(2) That a covenant was spontaneously entered into by the sinner to whom salvation had been thus joyfully brought. It was not a single impulsive act of gratitude, like the building of a church or the giving of £1,000. Such special overflowings of thankfulness on occasion of special mercies are very right and have abundant Scripture warrant, but the instructive thing in Jacob's case is that he engaged himself to a life-long and frequent *habit*.

(3) That in this vow the same proportion is named which his grandfather gave to Melchisedec. There is no other named in connection with giving to God; and it is evident this had got to be well understood generations before Moses.

(4) That the proportion is to be taken from, not luxury, but "bread to eat and raiment to put on."

(5) That it is devoted in direct recognition of the goodness of God in Providence and specially in grace.

* Compare Ps. xcv. 11, margin.

You may make a sermon for yourself from these five heads, and add the application.

5. Before we can leave the subject of Tithes, we must say something on that much-abused text, Mal. iii. 10: "Bring ye all the tithes into the storehouse that there may be meat in mine house, and prove me now herewith, saith the Lord of hosts, if I will not open you the windows of heaven and pour out a blessing that there shall not be room enough to receive it."

Occurring, as this passage does, in a prediction of the Messiah—the last prediction—and purposely couched in the style of Elijah and John the Baptist, one feels that we are getting away from Judaism at the other end. The cases of Abraham and of Jacob were long before Judaism: this, if not properly after it, has respect chiefly to the time and the circumstances in which it was to pass away. Those who would look for blessing and not curse at the coming of "the Messenger of the Covenant," must become honest toward God in the way of bringing all the tithes into His storehouse. For those who were under the law of Moses, it had, doubtless, a most literal meaning; for them, and for all others, its meaning is not doubtful, that honesty toward God requires a faithful devotement of a proportion of our income to His glory.

The special point in connection with this text is the promise contained in it. That promise is so very beautiful, and the need of its fulfilment is so deeply felt, that it has become a common-place phrase in all prayer-meetings. Thousands use the words who have no idea of where they are to be found, and that they are (if it were not that God is greater than their hearts) imprecating God's vengeance instead of entreating His blessing. "Prove me now herewith, saith the Lord of hosts." The promise is strictly bound up with our fulfilment of the condition. When we have conscientiously, as in His sight, settled the matter of what we ought to give to Him, and *have given it*, then we may with certainty expect the overflowing blessing—not till then.

I would only remark farther, that, while the promise of this text is fulfilled to individual Christians who observe the condition—fulfilled both in temporal and spiritual things—it seems a passage specially applicable to congregations and churches.

6. It remains now to speak of the degree in which these passages about the Tithe furnish us with guidance as to *the amount* to be given—as to what our proportion should be. It is a question of much interest to many who wish to be sincerely honest before God in this thing, and must be looked at in the light of the whole spirit and teaching of the New Testament. To the consideration of that teaching we are about to proceed; meanwhile the following more general remarks may be offered :—

(1.) The claim for religion and charity seems to be placed next after that for our necessary support. " Bread to eat and raiment to put on ; " having these, our father Jacob regarded himself as in a position to give to God. It is an extreme, certainly, to say that we should give everything beyond what will provide food and clothing, for many of God's children have been and are rich, and riches are promised as a blessing; but it is equally an extreme, and one into which we are much more likely to fall, to suppose that giving is not to begin as soon as we have food and clothing, but may be postponed until we have laid up something comfortable for ourselves. The maxim, " Charity begins at home," like " Honesty is the best policy," is a maxim of *this* world, and is worthy only of the god of this world.* "I believe it is quite true," said Sir Francis Crossley, "that if a man does not begin to give when he begins to *get*, or thereabouts, he will never begin to give at all." It is no secret that this true saying represents an experience of two generations, and is to be traced back to the training of a mother rich only in faith and good works.

(2.) The Tithe is a safe *minimum*. If one is guided not by the opinions of society around him, but by the Word of God, he will arrive at the conclusion that, however much more he may find himself able to give, he cannot well give less, unless under circumstances so exceptional that they should not disturb his estimate in this matter. If more than one tithe was exacted legally from the Jews, we, who enjoy the greater freedom of the Gospel, should acknowledge our superior privileges by giving at least as much to meet the greater need which God now has for our substance. And as for the examples of Abraham and Jacob, we cannot see how, in view of the seventh chapter of the Hebrews, any thoughtful Christian who prays over what he gives can content himself with devoting to God less than a tenth.

(3.) With all this, however, it is to be remembered that the patriarchal practice of tithe-giving was a matter of personal devotion, not of ecclesiastical law; the public exaction of a tenth *is* done away. Those who, like the followers of Edward Irving, make the giving of a precise tenth an ecclesiastical law carefully enforced on all church-members, vitiate the whole transaction, and run contrary to the genius of the Christian dispensation.

---

* "Tak ma word for 't," said an old Scotchman, giving advice to a youth entering on life; "tak ma word for 't, 'honesty's the best policy;' *I ha'e tried baith!*"

"Every man, according as he purposeth in his heart, so let him give; not grudgingly, or of necessity: for God loveth a cheerful giver." The highest form of law is the constraint of a thankful heart; to those who do not understand what that is, the New Testament says nothing touching this matter. We must have some fixed amount determined upon in our minds if we are to stand ready for giving at all times; and the tenth, being the only proportion of which Scripture speaks, may be safely taken as the unit of our sacred calculation, if we remember that the whole matter lies between our own consciences and our Redeemer, not at all between us and our church rulers.

For our first fundamental principle must never be forgotten. If any one is disposed to say, 'A tenth is too much; you would oppress us; we cannot afford it,' the answer is very simple. You have no occasion to argue and struggle for freedom from an irksome burden; no one is imposing a burden; God sets you perfectly free when He says that He loveth a *cheerful* giver. You are only asked to give at all on the supposition that you have been redeemed with the precious Blood, have been bought with a price, and are not your own; and these reasonings are addressed to you only as helping you to decide for yourselves how you may best carry out the gracious will of Him whom your soul loveth.

On the other hand, if any one is boastfully content with his giving of a tenth, and thinks he has thereby fully discharged all his obligations, and even made God his debtor, we would counsel him to read the parable of the Pharisee and the Publican, and then to take as his motto, if he can still do so, "I give tithes of all that I possess." (Luke xviii. 12.)

III. Before entering on discussion of the plainest text in the New Testament, we plead for sacred method and systematic habit in Giving from THE RELATION WHICH WE SUSTAIN TO OUR LORD JESUS CHRIST IN THIS MATTER.

That our giving does stand in some relation to Him is probably acknowledged by all; but how many are there who seriously think of the fact, and who have a clear understanding of what the relation is? We believe that if Christian people fairly brought this whole matter into the light of their relation to the Saviour, as redeemed by His Blood, as living daily under His eye and yet to be judged by Him, as His witnesses on earth, and as heirs of His glory, they would be led to adopt a sacred habit of proportionate giving even apart from the more specific injunctions of Scripture to that effect.

1. Think again of *His Example in John* xiii. 29. In addition to what has been said (pp. 168-169) let it be now remarked (1) That the purse of which Judas was the keeper was very scantily furnished. The proposal on one occasion to draw upon it for about £6, "two hundred pence" (John vi. 7), threw Philip into dismay. Yet there was *some understanding* among the followers and companions of Jesus as to the applications to be made of its contents, partly for their own use, partly for purposes of religion and charity, which is just the substance of what we plead for. (2) Judas was the treasurer. Why? The Lord knew what was in him, and gave him this office in order that *the habit* of administering their little fund under His eye might counteract the secret influence of greed. (John vi. 70, 71.) That part of the lesson will come before us again: it is the obvious habit, well-understood by His disciples, and in which the Master practically trained them so long as they were His companions, on which our attention should be fixed at present. Think-

ing of Him to whom we owe all, we think of a portion of His little store being set apart with forethought and love to be spent in doing good.*

2. Think of *His Eye.* Mark xii. 41-44. This text is full of instruction: it encourages the very humblest to give; it thus makes giving a universal duty and privilege; it proclaims a searching paradox as to more and less; and it requires us to feel that our givings are scrutinized by Him before whose judgment-seat we are to stand. Only this last point belongs to the present portion of our argument; but we may glance at the whole.

(1) The circumstances are instructive. It was the last week before His death, and Jesus was sitting in the second court of the temple over against the place called the treasury, where thirteen chests stood, each having a trumpet-shaped mouth, to receive the offerings of the worshippers as they passed in or out. The practice of thus gathering money for religious purposes, if nowhere expressly ordained, was at least ancient (2 Kings xii. 4-12); and while it is certainly one act of giving that is here specially honoured, we may note in passing that there is a measure of sanction tacitly put upon the practice of giving in the house of God,—giving often and

---

* The word rendered "Bag" is γλωσσόκομον, and occurs, so far as I can find, only twice in the New Testament, John xii. 6; xiii. 29. The lexicons give its original meaning as a "tongue-box, reed-case, for keeping the reeds or mouth-pieces of wind-instruments." Finding it used as a receptacle for money, one is fascinated with an idea of something neatly formed, safely fastened, the contents of which were well-arranged and carefully looked to. The best form of giving, according to some folks, is to take a little money carelessly from what is lying loose in the pocket and put it from one as a trifle; but what Jesus gave was taken from a carefully kept box, the contents of which were devoted beforehand to their several uses. If one may not press this as a matter of Greek criticism, he may at least be excused for finding a quiet delight in connecting the very receptacle of his sacred store with the personal habits of Jesus of Nazareth.

spontaneously, and giving in connection with religious privileges. For long, the stedfast eye was fixed on the moving throng. I remember no other time of similar silence during His abode on earth, unless it be that other "pause more full than speech" when He searched the consciences of the impure hypocrites. (John viii. 1-11.) Many came and went, heedless of that calm stedfast gaze, or marking with a scowl Him who had yesterday purged this His house; they are rich and cast in much; "they have their reward." But one came for whose coming the Friend of sinners, the Husband of the widow, had been waiting; she dropped into the Lord's treasury two very little coins, that her thankful heart might have some outget, that her deep poverty might not altogether exclude her from the joy of well-doing; then turned away with quiet thankfulness and trust toward the Father of the fatherless. *Now* will Jesus speak.

(2) But pause a moment, ere you listen to Him, over two words used to describe His scrutiny. He "*beheld*" —ἐθεώρει. It was not ordinary looking, still less the chance seeing of something unthought of till seen; but the searching of one who examines narrowly and with a purpose. When, in the parable, the king comes in to scrutinize the guests the same word is used. (Matt. xxii. 11.)

And He "beheld *how*," not *what*, they cast in. The amount was probably displayed by the self-righteous givers, and *any* eye might see that: the eye of the omniscient, holy, loving Saviour examines the state of heart from which the giving flows, and by which it is accompanied. Why? Because all giving of free-will offerings to God involves a solemn profession of gratitude to Him for His goodness to us in Providence and Redemption, and therefore supplies an obvious test of our true state before God. This is why giving is so solemnly associated with the final judgment. 'Does your giving indicate the love to me, wanting which any man is Anathema Maranatha? (1 Cor. xvi. 22.) Is it accompanied by such feelings of faith, good-will, self-denial, as to make it a laying up of treasure in heaven? Is it done unto me, because I, the Lord, have need?' Such is, in part, the searching force of this passage. Giving is a matter of free-will; there can be no doubt of that: so is repentance, so is faith, so is love, so is new obedience. What this text teaches us is that, while giving cannot be anything else but a matter of free-will, its quality must be such as to bear His scrutiny who "looketh on the heart." And our argument is, that in order to be able to bear such scrutiny we must first consecrate a proportion of our substance to God in Christ, and that, not once for all or at long intervals, but frequently.

(3) Notice carefully *what* the widow gave—" two mites, which make a farthing," "all that she had, even all her living." There were *two* mites, and she might very excusably have kept one: the whole sum was only a farthing after all, and many worthy folk would have said kindly enough, 'You had better keep it for yourself;' but it was in two pieces and she freely gave both, feeling all was too little for her love. I do not envy the man or woman whose heart is not keenly touched by this picture. She was depending on her Maker, who had promised to be her Husband, for the next meal, and she did not think that He would be angry with her for casting in these two mites. No: He was not angry with her! The mites represent some cheerful self-denial in a matter of food or firing, or a bit of extra work done: and the thrusting of this case upon their attention is a sore trial to those whose givings are always easy enough. It

is almost as sorely abused as that other text, Mal. iii. 10. One's disgust and indignation are roused by hearing persons whose givings have never cost them any self-denial, saying, "I will give my mite," or "I have given my mite." Brother! it is well for you and me that the Lord who has redeemed us is greater than our hearts and knoweth all things. If He were to take you now at your word He would say, 'There were *two* mites, and these were *all her living:* I have never proclaimed my approval of the giving of *mites* as the best sort of coin to give, but of *such giving as proves that the giver's heart is prompting him to give as much as he possibly can.* If you aspire to be like this friend of mine, you must look not to the smallness of the coin, but to the greatness of the gift.'

(4) Now we may be better prepared to understand what the Master means. "Verily I say unto you that this poor widow hath cast more in than all they who have cast into the treasury." More and less in the judgment of Christ are not the same as in our judgment: the smallest amount may be the best every way, may be even the largest, paradoxical as it seems. We are to regard our Lord as having chosen this extreme case for the purpose of impressing upon us the great principle that, however large a gift may be in itself, He does not receive it *unless it be large enough to prove self-denial on the part of the giver.* It is really outweighed by the smallest coin, a coin which only the poorest ever see and handle, if that be given in the self-denial to which the love of Christ constrains us. This is high doctrine; but consider whether there is any other meaning you can fairly put on the whole story.

More *to God* such an offering is than the easy offerings of superfluity. That is a golden saying of Ambrose (quoted p. 160 n.)—which may be fairly rendered thus —" God calculates the amount not by what is given *but by what remains.*" There is no proper sense in which God can receive our money merely as money, but He can and does receive the thankfulness, and the self-denial, and the prayer, and the trust; so that a very poor person, giving a mere trifle of which the world thinks nothing, is more in the way of giving really to God than one of easy circumstances giving a sum which looks well on a subscription list.

> "The censer swung by the proud hand of merit
>   Fumes with a fire abhorred;
> But faith's two mites, dropt covertly, inherit
>   The blessing from the Lord."

And who can tell but that such offerings are also " more " in respect of their efficacy, of the work done through means of them? Jesus would not work the miracle of feeding the five thousand until He had pressed His disciples thus—" Give *ye* them to eat," " How many loaves have ye? *Go and see* " (Mark vi. 37, 38); and the miracles consisted in multiplying what they, searching their stores and stretching their ability to the utmost, had given up for the purpose. The origin of many a great work on earth will be found, when we examine it, to suggest the same thought, that the Lord chooses rather to honour self-denial and love, by crowning their offerings with abounding fruits. One who is not much more than forty years of age said, at the close of a sermon, " I knew a lad in Christ once who adopted the principle of giving a tenth to God. When he won a money-prize for an essay on a religious subject, he felt that he could not give less than one-fifth of it. He has never since been able to deny himself the pleasure of having a fifth to give. God has wonderfully blessed that lad, and increased his means and his enjoyment of that luxury of luxuries—the luxury of doing good." There are other things, no doubt, that help to explain Mr Spurgeon's wonderful success in the Lord's work; but take note that this is one of the things.

Think, then, of the Eye of Christ upon us in all this matter of giving. You will in that case give with forethought.

3. And think of the *Glory* of Christ. Under another branch of the argument we shall consider the philosophy of the connection between our givings on earth and the glory we hope to enjoy with Him in heaven; for the present you are asked to look at the fact of such connection as plainly stated in Scripture. "A cup of cold water shall not lose its reward." (Matt. x. 42.) The parable of the unjust steward was told as teaching us that we may with "the mammon of unrighteousness make to ourselves friends who shall receive us into everlasting habitations." (Luke xvi. 9.) The last answer given to the rich young ruler was, "If thou wilt be perfect go and sell that thou hast, and give to the poor, and thou shalt have treasure in heaven." (Matt. xix. 21.) We can never forget how the Judge has placed the awards of the great day in most startlingly close relation to the uses men shall have made of their worldly substance. (Matt. xxv. 31-46.) He exhorts his little flock to "provide themselves bags which wax not old, a treasure in the heavens that faileth not." (Luke xii. 32-34.) And Paul speaks of such an employment of worldly goods as shall be "laying up in store a good foundation against the time to come, that they may lay hold on eternal life." (1 Tim. vi. 18, 19.) We ask, in view of the fact thus established, whether random, careless, impulsive, fitful giving, is likely to have such a

reward? Whether the very thought that the portion of our money which is given *may* have thus to do with the Glory of our Redeemer in heaven, and with our enjoyment of it, will not lead us rather to think over and consider the proportion that we give, and the spirit in which it is given?

> " Come let us join our cheerful songs,
> With angels round the throne,
> Ten thousand thousand are their tongues,
> But all their hearts are one.
>
> " Worthy the Lamb that died, they cry,
> To be exalted thus;
> Worthy the Lamb, our hearts reply,
> For He was slain for us."

Thus we sing. But part of the heavenly doxology is " Worthy is the Lamb that was slain to receive *riches* " (Rev. v. 12); and He does receive riches. It must be on earth that these are devoted to Him and spent for His glory, for we carry nothing out of this world. Surely, then, devout and frequent consideration ought to be given to the amount and the spirit of the offerings we bring to His feet.

4. The *Love* of Christ ought to move us in the same way. In the cases of the two boxes of ointment, what strikes us first and most is the warmth of passionate impulse; and they may well be looked on as warranting extraordinary givings on extraordinary occasions. But there was also in each case some forethought: the nameless woman [*] had considered what she might give to

---

[*] It is not well that the old Popish leaven should so far prevail as to lead many to think this was Mary Magdalene. There is, of course, no authority for that. On the contrary, one principal beauty of the story is that no name is told, and on the woman's part no word is spoken. Her name who, with weeping eyes and averted face, has held the gate of life open to so many thousands, will not be known until the Lamb's book of life is read.

Christ, and had brought with her from her home the most costly offering she possessed (albeit, when the fountains of the great deep of love in her broken heart were once opened, she gave Him an offering in His sight more precious, so that, after all, the costly alabaster was last and least); and the "very costly pound of spikenard" with which Mary anointed Him who had raised her brother from the grave, was, as we know on the best authority, laid by in store and "*kept against* the day of His burying." (Luke vii. 37-50; John xii. 1-8.)

These two fragrant examples, ever filling the whole world with a sweet savour of Him whose name is as ointment poured forth, are to our present purpose in two ways.

(1.) They instruct us that in giving to Christ we should consider how we may do our utmost. In both this was true; in Mary's case it was said "She hath done *what she could.*" (Mark xiv. 8.) No one can have earned the Master's approval thus, and truly done all he could, who has not brought into use the aids which forethought, method, and frequency supply.

(2.) They remind us that love is better than all. Without it, all methods, habits, and other appliances of Christian finance are of less than no value. It may be that, in our zeal for systematic giving, we are in some danger of losing sight of the love wanting which we will become, in this matter as in all other matters, "tinkling cymbals;" if so, let us often hear Jesus say, "Seest thou this woman?" and gaze both on Him and her till we feel how much we have been forgiven, and so, under the strong urgency of much love, strive to do all that we can.

THE BIBLE METHOD. 195

> " What though in poor and humble guise
>   Thou here didst sojourn, cottage-born ?
> Yet from thy glory in the skies
>   Our earthly gold Thou dost not scorn.
> For Love delights to bring her best,
> And where Love is, that offering ever more is blest.
>
> . . . . . .
>
> " Worthless and lost our offerings seem,
>   Drops in the ocean of His praise,
> But Mercy, with her genial beam,
>   Is ripening them to pearly blaze,
> To sparkle in His crown above
> Who welcomes here a child's, as there an angel's Love."

Let each of us thus take our giving into the light of our relation to the Lord Jesus Christ—His example, His eye, His glory, His love—and the result will be the forming and maintaining of *a gracious Habit*.

IV. We come now, having of purpose set these other considerations in the front of our argument from Scripture, to that passage which most definitely instructs us how the Church's exchequer should be formed and administered.

THE NEW TESTAMENT RULE IN 1ST COR. XVI. 1, 2.

Having regard to the design of this essay, it may be well to say something about the authority of these verses before we begin to expound them.

This ought scarcely to be necessary; but the development of doctrine in the Christian Church is very remarkable. Those who study that development will find that, from time to time, great truths (which have of course been lying in the Word since the canon was completed) have been only brought out, battled for, and at length universally received, after long centuries, according as the exigencies of the Church's and the world's history required. The doctrine of justification by faith, as contended for by Luther and Calvin, is one striking example. Another, more recent, is the teaching of Scripture in reference to Missions for the conversion of Jews and Gentiles. Within three-quarters of a century the obligation of the Church in the matter of such Missions had to be argued even in the supreme courts of our churches; and while there is happily no longer need for any argument in so far as Missions to Gentiles are concerned, it is to be feared there is still a considerable amount of crude thinking, and therefore latent unbelief, as to Missions to the seed of Abraham. A still more recent example is the doctrine of Christian Union, the teaching of Scripture concerning which began to receive any considerable attention much less than fifty years ago, and which, indeed, is as yet very imperfectly understood anywhere. But God is rapidly educating His people in this doctrine by the events of providence, and by leading them to closer study of His one text-book—always and from the first complete in itself. So that, even if it were more true than, happily, it is, that the doctrine of this text concerning a pure and effective Scriptural Finance is but newly discovered, that would be no serious objection to its authority.

Everything that can make a text of Scripture authoritative for us is here.

1. The word used is the strongest which the Greek language contains, διέταξα, "*I have given order.*" If you compare the use made of this same word in the eleventh chapter (ver. 34), where Paul is referring to the rectifying of abuses in the observance of the Lord's Supper, or in the ninth chapter (ver. 14), where it is said, "Even so hath the Lord *ordained* that they who preach the Gospel should live of the Gospel," you will

42

see that it would be very unnatural to give the word a lower meaning in this place, unless some strong and obvious reason appeared for so doing.

2. The only consideration which could warrant us to treat as not now obligatory a rule stated in such terms would be this, that there was something in the rule itself, or in the circumstances connected with it, to indicate a partial and temporary obligation. But the reverse is the case here. The "order" is given to "the churches of Galatia" as well as to those in Corinth and its neighbourhood; and the inscription of the epistle is, "Unto the church of God which is at Corinth, to them that are sanctified in Christ Jesus, called to be saints, *with all that in every place call upon the name of Jesus Christ our Lord,* both theirs and ours." (1 Cor. i. 2.) Nothing that looks like limitation there. Besides, in the next epistle, written a full year later, Paul refers again at length to this same great collection in terms which we are certainly not accustomed to understand with any limitation (2 Cor. viii. 9); so that it appears this rule had been in operation over all the churches of the Gentiles during all the Sabbaths of at least twelve months. It is, in fact, a sacred *habit* that the Word of God here inculcates, and a habit equally adapted to all peoples and all times.

3. No doubt the passage has reference to one special collection—that for the relief of the famine in Judea. But God had sent prophets into the Gentile Jerusalem to foretell that "great dearth" (Acts xi. 27-30); and it was reckoned to be worthy of an inspired apostle not only to be one of the bearers of the offering, but by his lips and his pen to stir up all the Gentiles to "prove the sincerity of their love" to Christ in the matter, and to guide them in the use of the wisest and most effec-

tive means. Why are such things made part of the Word of God at all, if not that they may serve as guides to Christian practice in all places and all times? When we are told how the churches of Christ were enjoined to go about the raising of money in one case, we are taught the general principle which is to be applied to the raising of money by Christians for Christian purposes in all cases.*

The authority of the text is thus clear; and we may be sure that before long time has elapsed it will be as little questioned as " Go ye into all the world and preach the Gospel to every creature." The fact that the churches of Christ in Europe and among the English-speaking populations of the globe have of late largely increased, and are, except in one or two limited spots, happily dependent for support only on the free-will offerings of the people, and the farther fact that, with the opening up of so much more extensive and rapid communications between nations, God has shed forth on His people so much of a missionary spirit, may well explain the greater prominence into which this rule has been recently brought. Still it would be a grave error to place it on a level with those precepts which have their witness in the natural conscience of the race, and to press it as an ecclesiastical law: its appeal is to the conscience of every enlightened Christian who is willing to be guided by the Word of God. And the appeal is of a more than usually urgent kind. It was not Paul who drew a line after the words,

---

* Though we have no particular respect for the authority of the Fathers, and are disposed to agree with the late Dr John Duncan in rather regarding them as children, Chrysostom's remark on the "every one" of this passage is of value as showing the estimation in which the rule was still held in his days at Antioch: "Every one, whether poor or rich, woman or man, bond or free—the handicraftsman, for instance, the sandal-maker, or the leather-cutter, or the brassfounder, or any other artificer—this I say as recommending a deposit (setting apart) of not less than a tenth part."

"Therefore my beloved brethren, be ye stedfast, immoveable, always abounding in the work of the Lord, forasmuch as ye know that your labour is not in vain in the Lord," and so robbed this rule of the weight it ought to have as coming immediately after the transcendantly glorious promise of the resurrection. The outcome of our reception of that truth is to be abounding work, and this is the first form of work mentioned.

Let us now make a fair and patient effort to understand just what the will of God is as taught in this memorable passage.

1. Perhaps the most obvious thing about it is that it supplies each man with a rule for calculating the portion he ought to give. It does not name any one proportion as that which each believer is to give—so far as the Word deals with that it does so elsewhere (see pp. 176-182); but it tells every man how to go about the discovering of the amount that he in particular ought to give: "EVERY ONE . . . AS GOD HATH PROSPERED HIM." No one is supposed to know this so well as the man himself, and at any rate no one but he is called on to make it matter of devout consideration. By this rule each of us is required frequently to remember the one source of our prosperity. There is constant need for such a reminder. "When thou hast eaten and art full, then thou shalt bless the Lord thy God for the good land which he hath given thee. Beware that thou forget not the Lord thy God, . . . lest, when thou hast eaten and art full, and hast built goodly houses and dwelt in them, and when thy herds and thy flocks multiply, and thy silver and thy gold is multiplied, and all that thou hast is multiplied, then thine heart be lifted up and thou forget the Lord thy God who brought thee forth out of the land of

Egypt, from the house of bondage . . . and thou say *in thine heart*, My power and the might of mine hand hath gotten me this wealth. But thou shalt remember the Lord thy God, for *he it is that giveth thee power to get wealth.*" (Deut. viii. 10, 14, 17, 18.) He who alone knows the forgetfulness and the thanklessness of our hearts has spoken thus. Under the old economy there was an institution for the express purpose of preserving in each heart a humble, grateful sense of the goodness of God. "And it shall be, when thou art come in unto the land which the Lord thy God giveth thee for an inheritance, and possessest it, and dwellest therein, that thou shalt take of the first of all the fruits of the earth, which thou shalt bring of thy land that the Lord thy God giveth thee, and shalt put it in a basket, and shalt go unto the place which the Lord thy God shall choose to place his name there. . . And the priest shall take the basket out of thine hand, and set it down before the altar of the Lord thy God. And thou shalt speak and say before the Lord thy God, *A Syrian ready to perish was my father,*" &c. (Deut. xxvi. 1-5.) This same purpose, of keeping alive in us a lowly tender sense of what we owe to God, will be served by the observance of the rule laid down. The man who frequently considers what he shall set apart for the purpose of giving, and begins his consideration by asking himself the question, How has God prospered me? will be in the way of fulfilling his own desire, "Bless the Lord, O my soul, and forget not all his benefits." (Ps. ciii. 2.)

How has God prospered *me?* That is a question worth pondering over often. "What hast thou that thou didst not receive?" (1 Cor. iv. 7) is a question very easy to answer in one sense, but by no means so easy to answer in another. It is easy—and of course it is correct—to answer, I have nothing that I have not received; but that is scarcely the answer it is intended we should give. Rather, pressed with the question, we should go over our position in society and in family life, our civil and religious privileges, our education, our bodily health, our sound reason, our *conversion*, particular answers to prayer, the strivings of the Holy Spirit in our hearts, the particular mercies of the past week—and against each we should write in our hearts, 'received from the mere favour of God in Christ to me a sinner' —and gaze at the reckoning—so full on the one side, only a blank as yet on the other—until we cry, " What shall I render unto the Lord for all His benefits towards me ? I will take the cup of salvation and call upon the name of the Lord. *I will pay my vows* NOW unto the Lord in the presence of all His people." (Ps. cxvi. 12-14.) The man who is in something like this spirit will, having the tenth before him as the general standard or unit of his sacred calculation, find little difficulty and no pain in fixing the portion of his substance to be set apart for the service of the Lord Jesus Christ.

For those whose incomes are fixed, whether paid weekly or at longer intervals, the ascertaining of the portion is obviously very easy : it may go on from week to week the same, with only now and then any occasion arising, from God having sent some special prospering, for the amount being increased, or from His having visited us with adversity (a rarer case and one the considering of which should be very carefully gone about) for the amount being diminished. But there are many whose incomes cannot be so easily ascertained : what are *they* to do ? We venture to offer to such two limits, always supposing they are honestly anxious to apply the rule "as God hath prospered me" to themselves.

(1.) *Err on the safe side.* What that is you must fix for yourself, and in doing so you may be helped to discover your own state before God.*

(2.) Ask yourself, How much do I feel myself warranted in spending on my dress, my table, luxuries (if any) such as tobacco and drink, entertainments, cab-hires and omnibus fares, newspapers, and the like,—even although I do not know my income exactly?

The essential thing under this first aspect of the rule is that we look at the question of how much we are to give sincerely in the light of what God has done and is doing for us. While a habit will soon be formed of setting apart the same coins in a purse or marking off the same sum in a book—a habit of the utmost value in itself—we must be on our guard not to lose that honest, humble, thankful regard to the goodness of God our Saviour, without which the mere habit would become a snare.

2. FREQUENCY is an important element in this rule; if we observe it we shall consider what we ought to give to God not seldomer than once a week.

Of course it is better that men should consider how God has prospered them, and determine an amount to be set apart as treasure for Him once a month, or once a quarter, or once a year even, than that they should never do it at all; but that is not what our rule says. "*On the first day of the week*" means *every* first day of the week. It means more; but let us limit ourselves to this idea in the meantime.†

---

* See further remarks on this subject under the head "Objections Answered," pp. 240-242.

† Κατὰ μίαν σαββάτων would not be fairly interpreted as meaning only that the Lord's Day is a suitable time for making this sacred calculation *when made at all.*

The call to such frequency of consecration is in full accord with the tenor of Scripture. From whatever other source we may obtain monthly or yearly supplies we do not get these from God. He may shew us a secure source from which all we need may come for the next fifty years, but He does not give us any guarantee that we shall live to enjoy that provision. On the contrary He obliges us, first, to live in hourly dependence on Him for health; and farther, when health is given He obliges us by the law of appetite to return more than once a day to the use of food for the mere supporting of life; and yet farther, for at least a fourth part of every day He lays us to sleep, so that we are not even consciously doing anything towards our own support. When He had just raised a girl twelve years of age from death, and while all were wondering and rejoicing about her, as if sickness and death were never to be thought of in connection with *her* any more, the Lord Jesus recalled them to a sense of their dependence by "commanding that something should be given her to eat." (Mark v. 43.) So far from encouraging the man of robust health and easy means to consider his future more secure than that of the most helpless victim of disease and want, He rebukes the disposition to say, "Soul, thou hast much goods laid up for many years; take thine ease; eat, drink, and be merry," as guilty madness: "Thou fool! this night thy soul shall be required of thee." (Luke xii. 19, 20.) An extremely common form of sin is described by James with startling fidelity:—" Go to now, ye that say, To-day or tomorrow we will go into such a city and continue there a year, and buy and sell and get gain. Whereas ye know not what shall be on the morrow. For what is your life? It is even a vapour that appeareth for a little time and then vanisheth away. For that ye ought to say, If the Lord will we shall live and do this or that." (James iv. 13-15.) The weekly review of all God's blessings, with the purpose of consecrating a portion to His service, would powerfully counteract this evil, and bring our lives more into harmony with the prayer which the richest needs to offer not less than the poorest, " Give us day by day our daily bread."

There is something deeply suggestive in this call to set apart money for God's service every week. God has taken the seventh portion of our time, and solemnly consecrated it to Himself, and said "Remember." Why? That all men may feel and acknowledge their dependence on Him for every hour, every moment. On the same principle does He ask that a definite proportion of our substance shall be given to Him, and that the relation of this part to the rest of our substance shall be looked at once a week, in order that we may realise and express our dependence on Him " who giveth us richly all things to enjoy." (1 Tim. vi. 17.)

When we come to speak of the advantages flowing from observance of this rule, we shall have more to say about this important point. You may, however, as well take note at once that such frequency and regularity would enable all, from the receiver of weekly wages up to the very richest, to earn His approval who said, " She hath done what she could." Scarcely anything else will enable the poorer to come up to the full measure of their ability: and nothing will have so powerful a tendency to save the richer from that subtile form of self-deception which consists in regarding considerable sums given at longer intervals as the giving of much. £5, in an annual subscription, men will persist in regarding as much: but half-a-crown a week is a considerably larger sum at the year's end. The former is apt to be what J. D. Burns calls "the censer swung by the proud hand of merit:" the latter is more likely to be "faith's two mites, dropt covertly."

3. There is, however, much more than frequency of giving required. Not any day of the week may be taken for this consecration, but THE FIRST DAY OF THE WEEK. Divine wisdom and grace are conspicuous here. That our storing "the Lord's portion" shall form part of the exercise of the Lord's Day is so essential a feature in the sacred method for which we plead that we crave your careful and candid attention to it.

(1) There is a high moral fitness in making the consecration of our substance to God part of the employment of the Sabbath. Not to mention the hour, which is but a useful invention of man, there are four divisions of time of which God is the Author. They all bear unmistakeable traces of His goodness: but three come from the God of nature, and are as obvious to the heathen as to those who enjoy the light of revelation. These are determined by the motions of the earth and its relations to the heavenly bodies in their motions: the light of the sun makes the day; the light of the moon makes the month; the regular succession of spring, summer, autumn, winter, fill up the rounded year. But what has created the week? On what permanent and universal fact does it depend? The will of God, apart from any obvious natural law, has given us the Sabbath, in order that we may directly connect it with Himself: and the fact on which it depends is the finishing of God's work, first in the old, then in the new, creation. The first day of the week is God's perpetual Sabbath,—the day being changed by the fact that the Son of God was still

wrestling with the powers of the grave on the seventh day, but "entered into His rest" on the first; by His own repeated consecration of this first day after His resurrection (John xx. 19, 26); and by examples of its observance in the Apostolical Church, of which this is one. (Acts xx. 7; Rev. i. 10.) We do not turn aside to argue this matter, but pleading with those whose best experiences have proved to them that the first day of the week is indeed the Lord's Day, we say, Is there not a most excellent fitness in conjoining the sacred storing of our substance with this sacred division of our time? Here is a duty, a privilege, purely spiritual and gracious. Nature can neither determine for me the proportion I am to give nor furnish motives why I should give at all: grace—the grace of the Lord Christ —alone constrains me in considering the amount, the frequency, the whole method, of my giving. As it is purely out of regard to the will of God in Christ Jesus, and to the benefits He has conferred on me, that I consecrate to Him the seventh part of my time, so it is as a believer in the Lord Jesus Christ, and under the same sense of the infinite value of Gospel blessings, that I devote to Him this proportion of my income. God claims a fixed proportion of my time to be given to Him at stated and frequent intervals, and in giving that I acknowledge Him not only as the God of my life, but much more as my Redeemer. God claims a fixed proportion of my money to be devoted to his service on earth, and in giving that I acknowledge Him not merely as the God who has bestowed on me all I possess, and has cast around my property the fiery shield of His commandment "Thou shalt not steal," but much more as Him who has loved my soul and given His Son to be my Saviour from sin. Is it not then highly fit that these two acknowledgments of the God of all grace should thus be associated ?

(2) Again : Our minds and hearts *ought* to be on the Lord's Day in the frame most suitable for giving. At other times the lawful business, or the equally lawful pleasures, of daily life are engaging us ; but now, on the first day of the week, secular employment has ceased, secular thoughts are banished, and we are occupied with the word and work of the Lord Jesus Christ our Saviour. The motives under which we should give are, for one, that " we know the grace of our Lord Jesus Christ who, though He was rich, yet for our sakes He became poor, that we through His poverty might be rich ; " and for another, that we are " considering the poor." (Ps. xli. 1.) When, if not on the Lord's Day, will the power of these motives be felt ? If the duty and privilege of frequent giving be recognised, no time can be found on which that duty will be better discharged than the first day of the week.

(3) We have spoken almost exclusively of that personal and private devotement of substance to God, which forms the hidden spring of the Church's Exchequer ; and indeed that is the matter of chief importance. (To see that the well be filled and kept full by a sufficient number of pure springs, however little each may be, is the principal concern ; the distribution of the contents of the well is also important, but what if there be nothing to distribute? or if what there is be not clean ?) Here, however, in thinking of the Lord's Day, we cannot but remember that on it the application of the sacred store is to a large extent made. " Give unto the Lord the glory due unto His name : bring an offering *and* come into His courts." (Ps. xcvi. 8.) The custom of our churches most properly connects the very entrance into

God's courts with an act of giving; and scarcely any one thinks of taking his seat in a place of worship without having first performed this act. But how is it performed? The amount may or may not be what it should; but what of the spirit? Those who at home have first "given the glory to the Lord which is due" will be in a position to "bring an offering" truly to Him. We believe the Church's Exchequer is impoverished through undevout and unsystematic giving: what if its contents are also unblessed! There is a constant danger in this mammon-worshipping age of our suffering money to secularize religion: but if this golden rule were observed, if all our tithes were at least "set apart" under the hallowing influences of the Lord's Day, whether they then pass from our hands or not, religion would be more likely to sanctify money.

4. We have assumed throughout that the giving of the Lord's portion is in the first instance a purely private and personal act,—the giving to any public fund, or to the needy, coming after. It may be as well, however, to give articulate prominence to this feature of the rule, "*Let every one of you lay by him*" (παρ' ἑαυτῷ τιθέτω). Not after the collector has called, not when brought into contact with want and misery, not when sitting under an earnest missionary appeal, least of all when a subscription-book, containing names we know pretty well, is thrust in our face, are we to begin to think how much we can give to God. There is very little chance in these circumstances of our giving anything to God at all; we will give to man, or to that incomprehensible abstraction we call "a good object," and probably not in a very earnest spirit. The very essence of this whole matter lies in the act being one of personal devotion—devotion in a fuller than the usual sense, both devoutness of spirit and

devoting of substance. The transaction, as we have shown (see at p. 174 and at p. 187), is one in the first instance, and chiefly between the believing soul and the Searcher of hearts—not the less the Searcher of hearts that He is our Friend and Saviour : and with this the language of our rule fully agrees—" let every one of you *lay by him.*" The feeder of the Church's Exchequer is " the Bag," (the Glossokomon)—mark this well. Those who are daily handling large sums of money will probably find the most effective and convenient form of " setting apart " the devoted sum, to be marking it in a book—like that banker in Philadelphia who had, or has, a page in his ledger mysteriously headed " O. P. J." (Old Patriarch Jacob) ; but most of us will find the keeping of a " bag " necessary to perfecting our consecration.

5. Another word in this text must be expounded. It teaches us that in our weekly consecration of a portion to sacred uses, we are to have respect to THE LAYING UP OF TREASURE IN HEAVEN. We found this remark on the word rendered " *in store,*" θησαυρίζων. It is common to understand this as referring to either a public or a private store, in which the money set apart by each on the first day of the week was allowed to accumulate until Paul should come for it. Perhaps there is no objection to that interpretation (although it does seem rather superfluous to tell those who have " set apart by themselves," or " each laid by him " his appropriate sum, to find another earthly store for it) : but surely a better interpretation is not far to seek. The word instantly reminds us of frequent sayings of the Lord Jesus, wherein He taught us to connect our present actings, and this particularly, with the spiritual and eternal realities,—sayings wherein He employed this very word : " Give to the poor and thou shalt have *treasure* (store) in heaven ; "

"Provide yourselves bags which wax not old, a *treasure in the heavens* that faileth not, . . . for where your *treasure* is there will your heart be also." (Matt. xix. 21; Luke xii. 33, 34). It seems to us far more likely that the Holy Spirit was bringing such language of the Master to Paul's remembrance while he wrote, than that Paul was thinking only of an earthly store. And our opinion is strongly confirmed by finding that in another passage Paul uses this word certainly with the heavenly meaning. "Charge them that they do good, that they be rich in good works, ready to distribute, willing to communicate, *laying up in store for themselves a good foundation against the time to come, that they may lay hold upon eternal life.*" (ἀποθησαυρίζοντας, 1 Tim. vi. 17-19).

Whatever may be thought of this exegesis, there can be no doubt at all that in every case in which the storing of money for God is rightly performed on earth, there is also, and at the same time, a laying up of treasure in heaven. Those who, like Mary and our nameless sister and the widow, are, in the fulness of their love to the Lord Jesus, doing this most truly, may also be least conscious of the fact: but it is the fact, nevertheless, and it behoves us all to understand it and lay it to heart.

6. This rule is UNIVERSAL: "*Let every one of you.*" No doubt Corinth was one of the richest cities into which Christianity had penetrated, equal with Antioch, and these second only to Rome. But it does not by any means follow that the converts were rich. There is a text, is there not, that says, "Ye see your calling, brethren, how that not many wise men after the flesh, not many mighty, not many noble are called?" Why, that text is in this very epistle, chapter 1st, verse 26th! Through persistent strength of worldliness we fancy a

primary qualification for giving must be the enjoyment of a comfortable income. The independent poor (using the word in its common meaning as including many who are above positive destitution), regard the proposed exemption as an insult; and they well may. While some may intend only kindness, the motive of others in not encouraging the poorer to give is, we shrewdly suspect, by no means praiseworthy: the widow's *two* mites are the most searching exposure, and the most solemn condemnation of easy, ostentatious giving. At any rate, this rule should warn us that, in proposing to draw any line, we run the risk of condemning those whom the Master praised, and quietly placing at His left hand those who need not be there but for their poverty! No: the divine method is precisely adapted to enable those who have least to attain to the highest measure of their ability in giving, by giving every first day of the week; and to the highest measure of blessing, by giving indeed to God Himself.

Those whose means are greater *can only be equal with them and no more*, and their abundance is apt to hinder them even in this.*

---

* In order to complete the exposition of this passage we should have spoken here of the words, "*that there be no gatherings when I come,*" but we reserve what is to be said about these till we come to treat of the advantages to the Church flowing from observance of this rule, p. 230.

CHAPTER III.

ARGUMENTS FOR THE CHURCH'S EXCHEQUER.

It might, in one sense, be held to be enough that we have set forth the fundamental principles of Scripture with regard to giving, and that we have proved from the same supreme authority the duty of consecrating a fixed proportion of income to God, and of each Christian by himself making this consecration every Lord's day. Had we not found these principles and this method in the Word, we could not have pleaded for them at all. But it is well to add farther pleadings based on the obvious tendency of a general adoption of this sacred habit to promote the prosperity of the Church, and on experience.

I. *The sacred method is productive of much good* TO THE INDIVIDUAL PRACTISING IT.

"The judgments of the Lord are true and righteous altogether. More to be desired are they than gold, yea, than much fine gold: sweeter also than honey and the honey-comb. Moreover by them is thy servant warned; and in keeping of them there is great reward." (Ps. xix. 9-11.) All that is true of "keeping" the will of God in the application of money for His service.

1. The man who forms the habit of setting apart all he can every Lord's day, out of grateful regard to what the Lord Jesus Christ has done for him, will always have something to give, and will find he can give it pleasantly.

The calls made upon us now-a-days are frequent, and sometimes sudden. The man who has never thought of making himself ready beforehand, whose givings must be taken out of his spending income, or (what is less agreeable) out of the sum he is laying up as capital for the future, must have difficulty in meeting these calls, and can scarcely meet them aright. Either he gives grudgingly, because he finds it not convenient at the time to give at all; or he gives recklessly, with an uncomfortable feeling that perhaps he ought not to give so much; or he says, So many calls come one after the other, I have nothing left, and so refuses. The man of a warm, impulsive disposition may often give more than he can afford, if he never considers the matter till it is too late—that is, till some call is pressing on his heart. In a prize-essay on this subject published in America many years ago, we find the following sentence; "One excellent minister's wife said that she rejoiced that her husband had adopted this rule, because she was now sure that his gifts would be regulated by his deliberate judgment, and not exceed his ability." It is probably on the other side that most will err; but why err on either side? Having a fund set apart expressly for giving, and which cannot be used for any other purpose, you cannot grudge what goes from it; and that fund being replenished weekly, it can never be long exhausted.

Of course there is room and need for consideration and common sense in administering the exchequer. We make no pretence to do more than lay down general principles, and state a particular habit: the giver must judge for himself as to the order of urgency belonging to the claims of his congregation, the poor, local missions, foreign missions, and so forth; as to the amount to be given to each; and as to how he is to adjust his weekly method to the giving of sums for which he is asked only once a quarter, or once a year, or once for all. But such adjustment will not be difficult *once the sacred habit is formed;* till then it *will* be difficult, indeed we cannot well see how any satisfactory adjustment of these points is to be made at all. If any reader feels difficulty in adopting the method for which we plead on account of his being required to give larger sums, and these at longer intervals, we would venture to assure him that instead of finding himself hindered in the giving of these larger sums, he would find himself considerably helped.

For (1) the greater number of our givings, and those involving the largest amounts for persons of ordinary income, are, or ought to be, *weekly.* The church-door plate gives the opportunity of making all the payments for support of ordinances in our own congregations that are of an ordinary kind. If in any place the element of pew-rents still remains to disturb the natural working of the free-will offering, the systematic giver can allow the sum to accumulate for twelve weeks, until the time comes when a revolution can be effected, and this imperfection is removed. At any rate, the man who has tried systematic weekly consecration honestly for a year, will discover that he can pay his quarterly pew-rent more easily than when he had no system at all.

(2) The same will apply to monthly collections, such as those for the Sustentation Fund, and even to those which are yearly, such as for missions. While scriptural principles are still but imperfectly understood and applied, the enlightened and conscientious giver must take the trouble, not very great, of allowing the weekly sums for these purposes to accumulate in his own hands; and he will be surprised and delighted to find that not only is there no difficulty in finding the monthly or yearly sum, but that he thus gives a larger amount, and

gives it with ease. Boxes furnish the simple means of this secondary storing for those (by far the larger number) who are accustomed to spend all that they do not give.

(3) As for the giving of large sums, and for special purposes, it is only, of course, persons of larger means who can give these; and the habit of devoting a proportion to God, and of considering this every Lord's day, will materially facilitate such givings.

We have already mentioned the case of the late Mrs Isabella Graham of New York (p. 171). Her habit secured to her, when reduced in circumstances, something to give, and the same good conscience in giving as when her means were ample. Mrs Graham was not always poor; and when once £1,000 came into her hand unexpectedly £100 went forthwith into the Lord's store. Here was provision for some larger giving; the thousand pounds would probably not have yielded the hundred but for the lifelong habit. The present writer had on one occasion to do with a missionary undertaking for which £650 were required. The whole expense was double that amount, but after all had been collected that it seemed possible to collect, this sum was still needed. A person called on him and said he was prepared to give £302, 10s. on two conditions—first, that his name should never be known, and secondly, that the remainder should be subscribed. It *was* subscribed in a fortnight; and the institution thus provided for has flourished these eight or nine years. The explanation of so large a sum being given unasked was that special circumstances had raised the giver's income, and *the proportion must be devoted*. There are probably many such cases, though it is by no means desirable to make them locally prominent in connection with the givers' names.

2. The systematic giver is protected from unpleasant solicitation. Not from all solicitation, for wants must be made known in special cases, and collectors must go their rounds until the sacred habit becomes so thoroughly established that all can be trusted to bring their offering to the house of God; but from all unpleasant solicitation. When it has become known in the circle in which a man moves that he is a total abstainer, no one thinks of pressing him to drink wine; in much the same way, when it is understood that a man is one of those peculiar people who regulate their givings by a conscientious system of primary and frequent consecration to God, his principle will be respected, and all right-thinking persons will feel that it would be rude and improper to urge or expect him to give more than he has frankly and promptly offered.

On the other hand, a refusal to give you anything for your particular object is not the same painful discouraging thing from such a man as it is from another, since you believe he is giving in other ways all that he can. For our own part, when we have occasion to gather money for any particular purpose (which is not very often) we ask those only of whom we have reason to believe that they are systematic givers, knowing that if such persons have to refuse us—a rare case—we can take their refusal with entire good nature and retain our full respect for their character. It is no small recommendation of the method we plead for, that it would conclusively rid the Church of the nuisance of religious begging, and bless the relation between askers and givers.

3. The habit of sacred weekly storing will promote a man's temporal prosperity.

It will do so directly. The three causes on which, as

a rule, prosperity depends, are economy, integrity, and accurate knowledge of one's affairs. As for the first, the very wish to have always something wherewith to do a little good will keep a man from rash outlays and self-indulgent lavishness. As for the second, the man most likely to slip into acts of dishonesty will not be he who every Lord's Day has his heart turned toward the Searcher of hearts in the very matter of his use of money. And as for the third, this godly habit requires him to know how he stands.

While good for all, the habit will prove a signal blessing to those who have small fixed incomes, to the receivers of weekly wages, and to the young entering on life—a signal blessing, we mean, as respects its influence directly on their worldly prosperity. Mr Gladstone, writing a public letter under date Jan. 9th, 1865,* uses the following weighty words :—" I think the object of the Society (which I understand to be inducing men to give at least *some fixed proportion of their incomes*, such as their several cases may permit, to purposes of charity and religion) is one that may be legitimately adopted by all, especially by all Christians, *with the greatest and most beneficial consequences*. And although it is the religious character and effect of such a proceeding that has the first claim upon attention, I for one believe its results would be no less advantageous in a *social*, and likewise in an *economical*, point of view."

It will promote welfare in this world by bringing the blessing of the living God. "The blessing of the Lord it maketh rich, and He addeth no sorrow with it." (Prov. x. 22.) The habit for which we plead is essentially a "seeking *first* the kingdom of God and His

* To the Secretary of the Systematic Beneficence Society, published in the *Benefactor* for May 1865.

righteousness," a habit of "godliness;" and the blessings promised may be confidently expected to rest on its faithful observance—"all these things shall be added unto you," "godliness is profitable unto all things, having the promise of the life that now is." (Matt. vi. 33; 1 Tim. iv. 8.) The man who believes the living God of daily providence to be the God who has given him the "unspeakable gift" of His Son, summing in one pardon and a new heart and grace and everlasting life, and who therefore makes giving for His service a matter of frequent and devout consideration, is surely in the way to have these promises made good to him. Mark the words—"Honour *the Lord* with thy substance"—let it be done in truth to Him and not to man—"and with the *first fruits*"—not the superfluity, not the chance leavings—"of *all* thine *increase*"—not fitfully, and not keeping up the same fixed sum you were wont to give in less prosperous days—"*so* shall thy barns be filled with plenty, and thy presses shall burst out with new wine." (Prov. iii. 9, 10.)

It will occur to the thoughtful reader that if these promises receive anything like a literal fulfilment, and if there are any faithful givers alive, instances of the fulfilment should be within reach. So they are; and a sincere Christian, to whom this subject may be new, could not do better than begin to look them out. We would give to them, specially to the young, the counsel that a now sainted mother gave to her children—"Keep your eyes open, and you will soon discover that God is a living God." Enquire a little into the private history and principles of the most successful Christian people about you, and you will find that they, up to the measure of their Scriptural enlightenment, are observing these sacred principles and this sacred habit.

The case of Mr Spurgeon has been referred to already (p. 191); but it is rarely possible to refer to instances of the living in connection with a matter that belongs so essentially to the heart and the hidden life. It would speedily kill the grace of the habit and reduce it to self-righteous form, to make everyone's systematic giving a matter of parade and gossip. Surely there were others in Jerusalem, although comparatively few, who were giving "much," according to the judgment of Christ, and whose hearts He saw and comforted; but He fixed attention only on one poor widow, and her name is not told. Probably the best form in which to put this evidence from experience and observation is: (1) To challenge the production of a single case of injury arising from loving, faithful, intelligent observance of the Bible rule; (2) To pledge one's own knowledge of uniform blessing, as everyone who speaks or writes on the subject will be able to do, if he is in a position to speak or write at all; (3) To present well-authenticated cases, when this can be done without injury to the individual concerned. For example:

From year to year, sometimes oftener than once a year, the present writer receives a golden sovereign in aid of the Gospel in Italy, from a family which many would class among the poor, the bread-winner being a mechanic not always in good health. This used to be brought by his aged mother: since her death it is brought by one whom he has brought up as "his own daughter." (Esther ii. 7.) On one occasion, hearing that he had been months out of work, we took an opportunity to inform him that we had been entrusted with a little money for relieving such, and that it was at his service. He thanked us warmly, promised to avail himself of the money whenever it might be necessary, but said that in the meantime they could get along. He has never needed man's help, and his mother has gone to glory richer than a queen.*

Two sisters lived together. Lucy went to a prayer-meeting on the first night of a new year: Mary stayed at home. Lucy in church and Mary at home were simultaneously convinced by the Holy Spirit that Mal. iii. 10 was a text which should be at once applied by themselves in the way of setting apart for God a tenth of their little income. When Lucy got home she would not allow Mary to speak till she had poured out to her her fresh conviction, and, when she had done, was astonished to find that her sister, alone at home, had arrived at the same conviction. Their neighbours ere long began to think the Misses Alport had had a fortune left them, so happy were they and so freely did they give. When a year of sickness and extra expense tried their faith, and made them consider whether they should reduce the proportion given, or take from their small capital, the post brought them the precise sum required.†

George Müller, himself an illustrious example of

---

* Our readers are, we must suppose, too intelligent to fancy that any such blessing can come if the spirit of bargain and greed enters into the transaction,—if money is given not for the purpose of doing good, but for the sake of the expected return. A story is told of a North-Highland family resident in Manchester. The husband, Dugald, went to a missionary meeting, taking with him a shilling for the collection; but his heart was so moved by what he heard that he went home in haste, took the whole five pounds he and his wife had saved for a rainy day, and gave it all. Flora's heart was not so warm, and she sometimes grumbled; but Dugald was always sure the Lord would never suffer them to want because they had given to Him. At length, an unlooked for sum of £500 was left to the worthy man, who then said, "Noo, Flora, I hope you're converted? See! the Lord has given us not only bread to eat and health to earn it, not only tenfold interest, but a hundredfold! Are you converted, Flora?" "Oh yes, Dugald, I'm sure I'm converted: but what a peety but we had given *ten* pounds!" Flora's conversion was very doubtful.

† God's Tenth. A Fact for the New Year. 23d thousand. London: J. F. Shaw & Co.

devoting money and all else in faith to the Lord Christ, told recently * a story of a poor woman, known to him, whose support was a little bit of ground planted with potatoes, who felt she must have the pleasure of setting apart a halfpenny a week for her Saviour. The potatoes prospered, and the halfpenny became a penny, and the penny twopence, and so on week by week, till now Mr Müller does not know how much she has the delight of giving.

4. But we have a stronger argument than any connected with this world. It is only with Christians we can rightly plead at all, and we urge them to adopt the sacred method of giving out of regard to the happy influence it has in promoting *spiritual* prosperity. This should touch us all closely, and you will not wonder if, conscious of the urgent need for every kind of influence that will raise the tone of vital godliness, we plead warmly.

(1) *Humility*, sincere habitual remembrance of what we are in the sight of God, is one of the rarest and most precious graces. This habit will powerfully tend to maintain it. A whole cluster of spiritual blessings is contained in truly and humbly saying, "Give us day by day our daily bread,"—gratitude, confidence in our Heavenly Father, relief from anxious care, thoughts of the time when we shall hunger no more. If it is your habit every Lord's Day to set apart a portion to God as a practical acknowledgment of His care and mercy, you will, under the blessing of the Holy Spirit, find yourself helped in keeping up the spirit of that daily prayer. An occasional and impulsive giving, having reference to a particular appeal presented by a fellowman, may or may not be accompanied by the *feeling* that all I have

* At a public meeting in Edinburgh.

comes from God, and that, in giving this, I am serving Him with His own: but if my giving be a habit, stated and secret, with which no fellowman has anything to do, but in which my heart transacts with God my Saviour, I am much more likely to feel as I ought to feel. "Who am I that I should be able to offer so willingly after this sort? for all things come of Thee, and of Thine own have I given Thee. For we are strangers before Thee, and sojourners, as were all our fathers; our days on the earth are as a shadow, and there is none abiding." (1 Chron. xxix. 14, 15.)

Though there were no other profit in it than the delivering us from that ostentation to which our hearts are too well inclined, and which there is so much in the customs around us to encourage, the method that requires us to look at our givings in the sunlight of the Cross would be of a value that cannot be reckoned.

(2) The right observance of this method *will enable us to lay up* "*Treasure in heaven.*" To the *fact* that there is such a thing we have adverted in pleading for the need of system and method (p. 192); now, in urging the advantages flowing from such method, we wish to arrest your thoughts upon the *philosophy* of the amazing fact. We fear thousands have never given earnest attention, or any attention at all, to the passages, so many, so plain, so startling, in which our Lord and the apostles connect our givings here with judgment and heaven. (Matt. x. 42; Luke xii. 21, 31, 32; xvi. 9; 1 Tim. vi.; Matt. xix. 21; xxv. 31-46; and others.) Look at these passages now, if never before. You ask, How can these things be? How is it possible that in any real intelligible sense these words can apply to *me* and to what *I* do in this matter of giving? My brother, you may be sure there is, whether you can find it out or

not, a very real sense in which each text applies to you; but after all, it is not obscure : you need only think a little and you will see it. First, *All deeds of real charity are to be revealed at the judgment.* It may be to the surprise of those who feel themselves "brands plucked from the fire," but not the less shall they hear the Judge say to them, "Inasmuch as ye did it unto the least of these my brethren, ye have done it unto me." EVERYTHING IS TO BE REVEALED: God forgets nothing: and in His book those deeds, however little in themselves and quickly forgotten by us, which were the outcome of a sense of the constraining love of the Lord Christ shall be found recorded—not, of course, as forming the meritorious ground of acceptance, but as the indispensable evidences of having felt that love and being joined to Himself by faith. Secondly, *Spiritual good is in its own nature everlasting.* Those who are converted are partakers of everlasting life, and are to dwell in the same heaven with those who have been the means of their conversion. Now obviously, in so far as your money, given in love to Christ and with prayer for His blessing, has been instrumental in effecting that transcendent result, *it shall be known to you in glory.* Not only here, nor here chiefly, is that word to be made true "Cast thy bread upon the waters; for thou shalt find it after many days;" and our Lord meant not irony (as some have strangely imagined), but plain truth, when He said, "Make to yourselves friends of the mammon of unrighteousness, that when ye fail *they* may receive you into everlasting habitations." (Eccles. xi. 1 ; Luke xvi. 9.) And you will still better understand this thing, and more closely feel the present connected with the eternal future, if you consider, thirdly, that *All true spiritual experiences are of necessity abiding.* A good conscience, victory over the love of the world, the joy of beneficence, the God-like joy,—these are of the very essence of the soul, and go with it wherever it goes. You see, then, what a real and tangible thing "Treasure in heaven" is. Consider whether this holy frequent consecration of substance on the Lord's Day be not the most likely way of laying it up. The question, when you withdraw it from the misleading surroundings of too common opinions and practices, and look at it patiently, prayerfully, in the light of the Master's words, becomes pungently simple; I must either be obeying Him, so that I have treasure and HEART in heaven, or deceiving myself by fancying my heart is in heaven while I am laying up no treasure there: in which way shall I be most likely to do what I ought, and to avoid what I ought not to do,—by giving fitfully, careless whether the amount and proportion be right in His eyes or not, from mere impulse, or according to man's judgment; or by humbly seeking to serve my Saviour by this sacred storing for Him?

(3) The habit will promote your soul's welfare by saving you from the greatest peril to which a professing Christian is exposed.

Can anything be more fearful to contemplate than the death of a covetous church member?—of one who, whether he has sunk into the degradation of a miser or not, has yet made this world his portion? *Then*, sin and death, heaven and hell, judgment and eternity, God and Jesus Christ his Son, hitherto but names to him, become urgent realities, while those other things, which alone he has treated as realities,—the world and its traffic, houses and lands,—become hollow ghosts that, though fading from his grasp, yet cannot be banished from his dreams. *Then* he does not go out of the world saying, "I would not live alway," but is dragged to his own place, "God *taking away* his soul;" and, unless the word of God be deluding us, it must soon come to this point. Who can endure to think of the horror of thick darkness engulphing such a soul! Who would not cry, "Let me die the death of the righteous, and let my last end be like his?" But if you shrink from such an end, you must do more than utter that cry; you must do something toward the realizing of your desire, and shun that "love of money which is the root of all evil." The man who so prayed had just been, with his own lips guided by inspiration, describing the blessedness of God's people (Numb. xxiii. 10); but after all he did not die the death of the righteous. Next to Judas, Balaam is the most fearful example of the damning power of covetousness. God rebuked his madness in vain, and he perished, loving the wages of unrighteousness. (2 Peter ii. 15, 16.)

Suffer me to reason with you a little upon this most unpopular of all subjects in the Christian Church, and to plead for the sacred habit as a means of escaping a danger from which it is not easy to escape. The love of money is *inconsistent with a hope of the soul's salvation.* Listen to the word of God in direct contradiction of the commonly-received notions of worldly-minded Christians. "Ye *cannot* serve God and mammon." "If any man love the world, the love of the Father is not in *him*." "Be not deceived: neither fornicators, nor idolaters, nor adulterers, nor *covetous*, nor drunkards, shall inherit the kingdom of God." "Ye know that no whoremonger, nor unclean person, nor covetous man who is an idolater, hath any inheritance in the kingdom of Christ and of God. *Let no man deceive you with vain words,* for BECAUSE OF THESE THINGS cometh the wrath of God upon the children of disobedience. Be not ye therefore partakers with them." (Matt. vi. 24; 1 John ii. 15; 1 Cor. v. 10, 11; vi. 9, 10; Eph. v. 5-7).

Turn not away in disgust, as though the mere suggestion of your being gathered with idolaters and impure persons were on our part a foolish and reckless insult. Who, as it respects character and profession, were they whom the word holds before us as warnings of the end of covetousness? Lot's wife, Achan, Balaam, Judas, Ananias and Sapphira, Demas: were they not regarded as worthy church members till God found them out? Each of them had a larger knowledge of saving truth than almost any who lived around them, and bore as fair a name as is borne by average church members. The truth is that the love of money is *peculiarly the church member's sin*. You can see how that comes to be the case. It is respectable; it is exempt from the rod of discipline which falls promptly on the sins with which the Holy Spirit has catalogued it; it grows secretly, and permits even the victim himself to remain in the belief that he is a good Christian; thus it is the chief means of destroying the souls of men *inside* the Church. "In what way are the professors of religion subject to this sin more than other men?" asks Andrew Fuller, and he answers the question with that penetrating sagacity which makes his writings so valuable—"As a fact, it has long impressed my mind, and I conceive it is not difficult to be accounted for. Supposing a person to be merely a professor, whatever impedes his evil propensity in all directions but one will be certain to strengthen it in that one. . . . If you wish to be thought a Christian you must not be a drunkard, nor a debauchee, nor a gamester, nor a liar, nor a blasphemer, nor an injurious person; *but you may love the world more than God*; for this, being confined to things between God and your own conscience, does not fall under human cognizance; or, though it may affect your liberality to men, yet, as the discipline of the New Testament leaves every one to judge of his own ability, and to give what he gives not as it were of necessity, but willingly, you may live undetected, and, *with a little management, unsuspected* by your brethren."* That is precisely how the matter stands; and if you shrink, as we hope you do, from becoming the victim of so ruinous a delusion, adopt the habit which most naturally tends to counteract it. The heart may easily deceive itself if our givings are irregular as to time, without regard to proportion, and only at the call of man. Self-deception will be more difficult if we give nothing to man that has not first been given to God, and if we make our giving to God a stated exercise of the Lord's Day. The late Mr Ross, who did more than any other man to inform and stimulate the public mind on this matter, used to tell us of a certain elder, with a great gift in prayer, but inclined to be narrow, who attended one of his meetings, and became convinced that whatever he gave he ought first to pray over. Being more than a mere professor, the next Sabbath he took the amount he usually gave and tried to pray over it, but could not,—doubled it, and still could not; and it was not until he had increased it fourfold, that he felt he could honestly lay it at the feet of his Saviour. This might have come in a little later to illustrate how the adoption of true principles would produce increase of funds; but it seems to us even more striking as showing how this child of God was gently delivered from a sin which needs to be burnt out of others in a furnace of chastisement. When Mrs Graham got that

* Fuller's Works, in 1 vol., p. 663.

£1000 unexpectedly (p. 215), she made the following entry in her diary—" Quick, quick, let me appropriate God's tenth, *before my heart gets hard.*" The possession of large sums is a great temptation. Such watchful self-distrust is the right spirit for a Christian steward to cultivate. In the case of one who had not the same godly habit, £25 might have been thought a very grand thank-offering to God; the heart would have been proud of making it, and God would have been robbed; in a word, the love of money and the pride of life would have got above the love of Christ.

II. The sacred method *promotes the welfare of the Church,* and *the glory of Christ.*

Under this head we gather four arguments. It would lead to happy change in the gathering of funds; it would increase the amount given; it would benefit the poorer members of the Church; and more blessing would rest on what is given.

1. The general adoption of this sacred method throughout the Church would lead to happy change in gathering funds.

The essence of the matter is, that the transaction shall be one not between man and man, but between the Christian and Christ—that whatever money is given to the poor, or to a congregational treasurer, or toward the building of a church, or to a missionary society, shall have been *first* given to God—that the amount of money I am to give is to be determined, not by prevailing custom, nor by what is asked from me, but by two other considerations, namely, What proportion of my income ought I to give? and, How has God been prospering me? Now, if all Church members, at least the greater number of them, were thus acting,—

All that is irksome about collecting would disappear. Too often at present the work of the collector is not collecting, but begging; he (oftener she) has to use arguments to induce the person solicited to give at all, or to give what in his or her judgment is an adequate amount; and the proceeding is highly unpleasant to both parties. All this would be changed. In the case of stated contributions, such as those for the support of the ministry in the Presbyterian Church at large, the collector making her monthly visits will find the money ready and willingly given; after a while it may even be found that the monthly visits are not necessary, that the sums are brought in faithfully to a congregational treasury for the purpose.* In the case of occasional gatherings, the money will either be given freely, or if there is none to give, the collector will understand that it is not grudgingly withheld.

Those givings, the amount of which is at present fixed by our fellow-men, would be exchanged for free-will offerings. If the principles we have been expounding are scriptural and right, this change must come. Without going into the whole question of pew-rents—largely agitated outside the Presbyterian Church as well as within it—we point to two circumstances inseparable from them: (1) The amount is fixed and always the same, for richer and poorer, from one year to another. (2) That amount is formally assessed and collected by our fellow-men. These two things are sufficient to condemn the system, of which they are necessary elements. We cannot see how any one who is persuaded of the new

---

* The sooner this comes to pass the better, for knowledge by fellow-men of the amount we give is a weakening element. While not advocating the rash overturning of existing methods, we must not let the statement of the perfect theory be marred by accommodating it to these methods.

method being according to the genius of Christianity and the teaching of Scripture, can defend pew-rents *in theory*. As a matter of practice, their removal must be brought about by diffusing sound information, and inducing individuals to adopt Sabbath storing; and towards this the efforts of those office-bearers who have become convinced that there is a more excellent way should be wisely and earnestly directed. For years there sat under our eye in adjoining pews two men, the one with a large family grown up, the other with little children—the one having a fixed income of £200, the other spending £2000; yet the sum paid by each was the same—in the one case probably a burden, in the other a trifle. But such inequality is a small evil in comparison with that which arises from the transaction being so directly a transaction between man and man. That which ought to be *giving* is turned into *paying*. The spirit of bargain comes in where it ought to have no place whatever; the grace which should pertain to the supporting of the house of God is destroyed; and the mass of Church members are led to deceive themselves by imagining that they have been doing something well-pleasing to God when they have only been dealing with their fellow-men. We earnestly urge the adoption of the Church's Exchequer according to Paul's teaching, because that would deliver the Church from what is at present a serious hindrance to the exercise, by the greater number of her members, of truly Christian feelings and principles in the matter of giving.

These remarks refer to the stated and ordinary support of Christian ordinances. The benefit of the Church's Exchequer would be equally felt in connection with special efforts. "*No gatherings when I come.*" Paul had, it would seem, some unpleasant experience of forced, fitful collections, dependent on his presence; and is earnest against these. There is no objection, but the reverse, to preaching public sermons on behalf of great Christian objects, whether special or stated. Such sermons are highly useful in the way of informing and rousing the public mind and heart of the Church; but there is a serious objection to making the givings of Christians dependent on the transitory excitement connected with these sermons and with annual meetings. Benjamin Franklin was obliged by George Whitfield to turn his pockets inside out; but it would have been much better for Franklin, and for the cause of charity, had the great preacher persuaded him of the duty and advantage of setting apart something for the service of God every week to the end of his life. Our plan is to lay hands on Paul, Apollos, Barnabas, every eloquent and gifted preacher, and turn him into a machine for raising money. Paul says, and is guided by the Holy Spirit in saying, 'Do it yourselves, rich and poor of you, in your own closets; do it by littles every Lord's day; do it so as to get for yourselves the good of doing it, and the fair credit of being faithful stewards of the manifold grace of God. Do not degrade yourselves by needing my appeals to force your liberality, nor me by compelling me to make these appeals. Let there be no gatherings when I come.' No doubt Paul is right; and when we make a change, and adopt his plan, we will find much ease and blessing.

Another kind of "gatherings" do not seem to have existed in apostolic days, else no doubt we would have had still stronger remonstrance against *them*. It does not appear that public sales of articles more or less useful, with the aid of brass bands, gay dresses, insinuating smiles, mock auctions, and profane use of the lot, were common in Antioch, or Corinth, or Ephesus. We do indeed know that Barnabas sold land, and Dorcas "made coats and garments," by way of advancing the interests of Christ's Church on earth; but they did this as privately as possible. Aquila and Priscilla, and Paul himself, were practical upholsterers; yet it never occurred to them to get up showy sales of their handiwork. They preferred to have it in their power to say, "Ye yourselves know that these hands have ministered unto my necessities, and to them that were with me. I have showed you all things, how that so labouring ye ought to support the weak, and to remember the words of the Lord Jesus, how He said, It is more blessed to give than to receive." Possibly they feared that, were they to adopt such methods, ostentation, rivalry, giddy excitement, and very doubtful honesty, would mar the simplicity of Christian giving, and deprive the givers of the benefits they should have received from a practical outgoing of love to Christ, by helping them to deceive themselves. *Their* counsel is, "Upon the first day of the week let every one of you lay by him in store as God hath prospered him, that there be no gatherings when I come;" and one very happy fruit of a general adoption of that counsel in the Church would be to rid it ere long of the shame and nuisance of fancy fairs for purely religious purposes.

2. This method, generally adopted, *would increase the amount given.* This in various ways.

(1) Congregational funds would not then suffer, as they do now, from sickness, seaside residence, and rainy days. The late Principal Fairbairn, presiding over a meeting held in Glasgow ten years ago for the advocating of these principles, said in our hearing that if the day appointed for a public collection throughout the

Free Church happened to be wet, the collection suffered to the extent of between five and six hundred pounds. This source of possible loss would be effectually stopped if members of churches learned to give first at home, and to Christ, not in Church only.

(2) The *frequency* of giving would have surprising effect in raising the amount. If you ask a man of limited income to give you 10s. for this object and 15s. for that, and 20s. for another—all about the end of the quarter or of the year,—he has to say, often very reluctantly, "I have it not," and to give a smaller sum, such as can with propriety be taken from the small amount which is at the moment in his hands. But if you get that person to form the religious habit of privately devoting a proportion of his income every week to the Saviour, he will rejoice, and so will you, to find how much more he is able to give and with how much greater ease. A gentleman in business, who used to give £1 a year to a missionary fund, a liberal man and doing more than many about him, found when he adopted these principles that he could with more ease put a shilling every Sabbath into his son's mission-box, a clear gain of £1, 12s. "With a short experience, and a rather imperfect one, I am a convert to the storing system, the magical power of which no one could believe unless he had tried it,"—so writes a banker.* We are persuaded that, taking rich and poor

* Some years having passed since the sentence referred to was written, I wrote to the gentleman alluded to, asking him to inform me of his present views. With his permission I give his letter, suppressing date and name, of course. It will interest and help earnest-minded men of business.—"Your note has interested me. I had entirely forgotten the sentence you quote, but your note has brought it vividly back, and the circumstances that prompted it. The experiment was a most pleasant one, but of short duration. I have aimed for a great many years at giving *a third* of my income to religious and charitable purposes, and I began to store on that basis. *Through bad management the store was*

together, and making the support of ordinances dependent on the weekly offering *alone*, instead of trusting to the pew rent, a startlingly larger sum would be realised; for then the poorer would find themselves enabled to give much more, and the richer would be saved from the self-deception of regarding half-crowns and half-sovereigns as really large *for them*.

(3) The *proportionate* principle would lead to remarkable results in the same way. The greater number of incomes are not fixed; the object of all men of business is that their incomes should be *growing*. Half a generation has produced an effect which it is not altogether satisfactory to contemplate in augmenting the national wealth. (See p. 160 and note.) The expenditure on luxury, often injurious luxury, is portentous, and forces one to remember that Babylon, Persia, Greece, Rome sank not through poverty but under the sheer weight of the precious metals, under the enervating self-indulgence produced by fulness. Spain, which in the days of Columbus was the richest nation of Europe, and the Republic of Venice, are more recent examples of the same peril. We have a conserving salt which these nations had not; but is it potent enough to keep the corrupting influences under? Let those answer

always overdrawn, for I have not been able to keep down my givings to that proportion. In self-defence and in defence of the system, I ought to say that throughout many years there have never been wanting *special* claims that seem to shut me up to pass the limit I had fixed. *God has mercifully prevented expenditure in other directions* which I thought it fit to anticipate, but was thus unable to provide for; so that, following what I felt to be duty not altogether welcome, I am not poorer to-day than I expected, while I hope some have been benefitted by what I have been enabled in my small way to do. *I hope, however, to return to storing*, and *to take into my counsels*, in distributing the store, *my children*, who are now becoming old enough to be interested and instructed thereby. *I feel that such a systematic education in conscientious giving ought to be fruitful of good works in them.*"

who are familiar with the social life of London, or of Glasgow, or of Belfast, and who have considered the effect of the general tone upon the lives of Church members. Obviously, if the man who last year made £300 and gave £30, makes this year £350, his principle of proportion will lead him to give £35. Simple adherence to the *habit*, without any pressure from the outside whatever, will in this way cause a steady, natural rise in the income of the Church's Exchequer. We have referred (p. 215) to a case in our own experience; and there must be many such cases. We know of a firm which began business with the principle of devoting a tenth of all profits to the Lord, besides what each partner might give of his own income; that firm has prospered, and of course the tenth has come to be a much larger sum; and one of the partners at least (possibly both) is now devoting *the entire proceeds* of the business, several thousands a year, to charity and religion. As the number of such cases increases (and it *is* increasing) the amount given to Christ will become larger and larger. We earnestly commend this aspect of the matter to practical men.

(4) The *freeness* of the giving will favourably affect the amount. The distinction is great between a gift and a bargain.* The natural disposition is, in the one case, to prove love by making the amount as large as

---

* The late Mr Ross never tired of expounding this. It was from another, however, that we heard the following story :—A worthy woman used to go every Saturday from the coast to a village a few miles inland selling fish. On one occasion, when she went into the general shop the shopkeeper said, "Ye see, Jenny, my hands are full o' customers; here's sixpence, jist go into the house and lay the fish down; and gie me them according to conscience." Jenny went, laid down first three fish, and then another as the thought struck her "Mr Broon's *trustin*' me to gie according to conscience." But next Saturday, when Mr B. said, "That was a grand bargain, Jenny; jist go in and lay them doon again," Jenny said, "Na, na, Mr Broon, I'll sell nae mair fish according to conscience! Come you and mak' a bargain."

possible; in the other case, to pay as little as possible. When you bring in pew-rents, treasurers, printed lists, collectors, between the Lord Jesus Christ and the giver's heart the tendency is, and alas! the *effect* very often is, that you prevent his conscience and heart from operating at all, and he gives just so little as will satisfy you or public opinion; and he gives it as a payment, not as an offering of love. The result is very different when the only Lord of the Treasury is Jesus Christ, and the only Chancellors of the Exchequer are a purged conscience and a broken heart. *Then* are given Abraham's and Jacob's tithes, *then* the fragrant alabasters are poured forth, then come in the *two* mites!

3. The sacred method *would do good to the poorer members of the Church.* The application of the method has been proved to be universal. If it were brought into universal practice

(1) *There would be fewer persons needing succour.* Those who are receiving small sums, in shillings, weekly, are exposed to great temptation to spend all. The sum they could lay by is so very small that it seems not worth while to begin. Then come petty debts, living beforehand, straitness, and (with one or two weeks' sickness or want of work) *real* want, quickly followed by the loss of independence and self-respect, never to be regained. This is the common history; the evil is want of frugality. There is no occasion for our preaching the possibility and the advantage of such persons acquiring habits of economy. Penny banks, clothing clubs, and benefit societies do that more effectively; but what we say is, that were they taught the use of this sacred habit, economy with its attendant blessings would be connected with the strongest of all motives—the love of Him who for our sakes became poor.

(2) And there *would be a larger number of persons* ready to help the poor. This is obvious.

(3) And the help would be more kindly and effectively given. Those who have most experience in this matter will agree with us that what is most needed is not that a larger amount shall be given for the relief of the poor, so much as that there shall be more of loving contact on the part of those who give the money. Will not those who have set apart their money in grateful remembrance of Him, who said "Ye have the poor with you always, and whensoever ye will ye may do them good" (Mark xiv. 7), be likely to look wisely and kindly after its application?

4. The sacred habit would benefit the Church by *leading to a larger degree of blessing on what is given.*

For ourselves, remembering the "*more*" of our Lord spoken in connection with the two mites, and considering facts, we are more impressed with this consideration than with any other.

We cannot but think thus :—If there are principles laid down in His word, and a certain proportion and habit taught in reference to giving, is it not likely that the Lord, who alone can bless, will mark His approval by granting richer and more abiding fruits to follow the money which is so given? Can the same amount of blessing be expected to rest on what is given in careless disregard of the principles and the method which He has taught? We know well enough, and are all orthodox enough to say, on occasion, that all our givings cannot produce spiritual results of themselves, cannot edify or convert souls : but it may be that we do not feel this as deeply, as constantly, as we ought. And in proportion as we do feel that obvious truth, we will be likely to try to please God in the principle and manner of our giving.

But we can go further than that general reflection. If our purpose in giving is to glorify God in Christ, and if we devote a proportion to Him, we will be likely to give *with humility*. Ostentation is a ruinous snare : yet how many temptations there are to it as things are! The names of large givers are paraded : one congregation boasts itself against another, one society against another society. It is little wonder if the living Head of the Church should rebuke a spirit so uncomely in sinners saved by grace by withholding His blessing altogether or in part.

And once more, those who religiously practise the habit for which we have been pleading, will *follow their money with prayer*. Say whether there is in the Church a due proportion of true, humble, fervent prayer to the collecting of funds. And say, Is the Giver of "every good and perfect gift," who has claimed as *His* the silver and the gold, honestly recognised, first, when the need of funds is felt? and secondly, when the funds have been got and are about to be applied? Now, anticipating the only answer which can be given to these questions, we urge the Christian reader to consider the advantage, in the highest form, likely to accrue to the Church from a *habit* of giving on Scripture principles. If a man gives out of cold formal custom, or to get rid of a collector, or for display, he will not think of his money again unless to see it acknowledged in a subscription list; but if a man gives out of what he has consecrated to the service of Christ, there is some probability that he will pray for His blessing on the congregation, on the needy one, on the mission toward which his money is given. At a meeting in London some years ago one of the speakers told of "a little girl who gave a penny to one of the large county associations of the Bible Society in England. The anniversary of the Bible Society in the county town came round, and the young giver determined she would be there to see what had been done with her money. Listening patiently through the reading of a long report, she was rewarded by hearing at the end of it—'There has been collected during the year £1656, 18s. 1d.,' and started up exclaiming, 'Oh! there's my penny!'" Of course it was just her penny, and she had a right gladly to connect it with all the blessings of Bible circulation, and we would not wonder if she should hear of that penny again in another place. If there were hearty interest and prayer in proportion to all the money given, certainly far more spiritual effect would attend our Christian agencies. Where conscience and heart have had to do with giving, so as to make it an act of faith, such prayer of faith will go with the money, and follow it into lonely garrets and to the ends of the earth.

CHAPTER IV.

OBJECTIONS ANSWERED.

So far as there is difficulty about the authority attaching to 1 Cor. xvi. 1, 2, that has been already removed; and, probably, enough has been said to silence those not very worthy objectors who say, "You would establish a system fitted to grind the faces of the poor." They should remember what the widow did with her last handful of meal, and how the deep poverty of the Macedonian Church abounded unto the riches of their liberality. (1 Kings xvii.; 2 Cor. viii. 1-3.) But a word or two may be said by way of meeting some other objections we have now and then heard from worthy people.

I. "*You propose a revolution.*" Why not? We have great respect for the wisdom of our ancestors, yet we do not follow them in everything—in forbidding Jews to buy and sell in the open market, in hanging sheep-stealers, in leaving the heathen without the Gospel of Christ. Is it absolutely necessary to follow them in a careless, imperfect manner of giving? If the arguments advanced here from Scripture and Christian expediency in favour of systematic, proportionate, frequent giving, be sound, so that the principles and the habit we urge you to adopt are proved, you will agree with us in saying that the vested interests of indolence and greed must not be allowed to stand in the way of reformation. We advocate no sudden, rash, unconstitutional innovation, no breaking down without a corresponding and a better building up; but the sooner, the more wisely, the more resolutely the Church sets herself to the work of this thorough reform of her Exchequer the better for all her own interests, and for the world.

II. "*But we cannot ascertain how we stand every week.*" In reply to those who urge this objection, not as an easy way of silencing a minister who knows nothing of business, but as an honest difficulty, we say,

1. Consider candidly again the argument in favour of weekly storing, and come to an unprejudiced judgment as to whether the thing be right in itself. If your conclusion be that it *is* right, we will trust you, as conscientious Christians, to find some way of bringing the exigencies of your position into harmony with the Master's will.

2. Consider what your weekly *expenditure* is (you must know that), and take it as a guide.

3. Candidly allowing that on this point I, being a minister with nothing but stipend for income, was not able to speak with much authority to men of business, I took the following course. Before committing myself, many years ago, to the public advocacy of these principles, I submitted this particular point to the judgment of several shrewd Christian men engaged about money, and received from them the unanimous assurance that the difficulty was one which could be quite well got over by those who honestly tried to get over it.* The following are wise words of a business man and a noble giver, the author of the last essay in "Gold and the Gospel" (by whom, we have been told, the expenses of prizes and publishing were anonymously defrayed. He has now gone to the Christian steward's reward) :—

"It is more difficult, indeed, for individuals to do so who are living on the profits of business. The scriptural precept, however, is not less incumbent on them, and the command of God coincides with their truest worldly interests; for a very large amount of the failures in business that take place, and the consequent losses and misery which are thereby entailed on the sufferers, their families, and creditors, may be traced to this omission. Whereas regularity in stock-taking, and in ascertaining the yearly amount of profits or losses, is a marked characteristic of a prudent tradesman. . . The first thing to be done, then, by those whose property is invested in business, is to find out what they have gained or lost since they last took an account of their

---

* I received the same assurance last month (Nov. 9, 1876), after addressing about four hundred office-bearers in Belfast.

stock. The next would be to strike an average of the profits of the two, or three, or more preceding years. In some occupations the gains are so regular from year to year, that such a process would be needless; yet in many trades the fluctuations are so great, from high to low profits, or from gains to losses, that an average of several previous years must be taken in order to ascertain the proper amount of profits on which to take a percentage for God.

"It is obvious that this is the only way of meeting the difficulty, for it would not at all be proper to be varying stated subscriptions every year, as profits may rise or fall—and it would be still less expedient to stop them altogether in years when there may be losses instead of gains; for, besides the injury which would accrue to societies thus precariously supported, it would be exposing to the world the good or bad results of a person's pecuniary transactions, which every prudent man of business is careful to avoid."*

III. "*You would turn charity into taxation with your proportions and fixed rules: we like to give impulsively.*"

As to the latter part of this objection, we have no doubt whatever that you like to give impulsively; but we might call such giving by another name and say, you like to give, *or not* to give, at pleasure. If impulse could be trusted to secure a sufficient amount to satisfy the Lord's great need, to stir you up to give on every occasion when you ought to give, and give the sum adequate to the occasion, all would be well: but this is just what impulse notoriously fails to do.

And as for taxation; we repudiate the charge with all our heart. (See p. 208.) Let every man assess himself in

* "Gold and the Gospel," pp. 356, 357.

the sight of God, but let no man venture to assess his neighbour. Such self-assessment is the only means of obtaining a good conscience and entire freedom. Having made your own assessment before God, you are independent of your neighbour's judgment, and are delivered from the deceit and selfishness of your own heart.

IV. "*Let not your left hand know what your right hand doeth.*"

This is Scripture; but all quotations from Scripture are not good arguments. Witness a certain quotation from the ninety-first Psalm, made on the pinnacle of the temple by one on whose side no one likes to be found.

The objection was made to us in good faith by a sincere Christian who feared the practice pleaded for might have a tendency to foster self-righteousness. Our answer is, (1) Let self-righteousness be guarded against in this as in every other good thing. It is *always a good thing* which self-righteousness fastens on and destroys. If this good thing be so perverted, that will only prove that the heart is deceitful above all things and desperately wicked—which was known before. (2) If any one matter of Christian practice has more tendency to counteract self-righteousness than another, it is this for which we have pleaded. That a man should form and maintain a sacred habit which requires him to be watchful over his manner of spending money, to practise self-denial, to make practical acknowledgment once-a-week of the divine omniscience and goodness, and to think how much he owes to redeeming grace,—is not surely likely to feed his carnal pride.

Let it be said, before we close, that intelligent right-hearted laymen can do more for this good cause than ministers can. Let them unite for the purpose of strengthening one another's hands,—(not, however, except in rare cases mentioning the proportion which each gives); let them scatter the publications in which the scriptural way of forming, feeding, and administering the Church's Exchequer is expounded; let them organize meetings and procure sermons for the purpose of making the exposition of true Christian finance more popular and more effective; and above all, let them be ready to avail themselves of every opportunity in conversation to expound the matter intelligently and warmly themselves.

The great hope of the good cause, however, is in the rising youth of the Church. Bible principles touching the holy use of money being imbibed while opinions and habits are forming, the sacred practice being adopted from the outset of life, as soon as they begin to handle money of their own, thousands of the young would be saved from temporal and spiritual ruin; the existing agencies for well-doing in the name of the Lord Jesus Christ would be maintained in unstraitened efficiency; fresh organizations would be formed; and the rain of the Holy Spirit would descend more richly upon all.

"Sow to yourselves in righteousness, reap in mercy; break up your fallow ground: for it is time to seek the Lord, till He come and rain righteousness upon you." (Hosea x. 12.)

TEXTS REFERRED TO.

	PAGE
Genesis xiv. 20	179
„ xxviii. 22	175, 180
Exodus xxxv. 5, 21	164
„ xxxvi. 4-6	164
Numbers xxiii 10	225
Deut. viii. 10-18	200
„ xv. 11	163
„ xxvi. 5	200
1 Kings xvii. 10-16	239
2 Kings xii. 4-12	187
1 Chron. xxix. 1-19	164, 175, 222
Psalm xix. 9-11	212
„ xli. 1	207
„ l. 12	175
„ xcvi. 8	207
„ ciii. 2	200
„ cxii.	163
Proverbs iii. 9, 10	175, 218
„ x. 22	217
Ecclesiastes xi. 1	223
Zechariah vi. 13	180
Malachi iii. 10	182, 220
Matthew vi. 24	226
„ vi. 33	218

	PAGE
Matthew x. 42	192, 222
„ xix. 21	192, 210
„ xxii. 11	188
„ xxii. 21	174
„ xxv. 31-46	192, 222
Mark v. 43	203
„ vi. 37, 38	191
„ xii. 41-44	160, 165, 187
„ xiv. 7	176
Luke vii. 37-50	194
„ ix. 58	171
„ x. 25-37	166
„ xii. 32-34	192, 210
„ xii. 19, 20	203
„ xvi. 9	192, 223
„ xviii. 12	185
„ xix. 31-34	175
„ xxiii. 50	165
John iv. 8	168
„ vi. 7	186
„ vi. 70, 71	186
„ viii. 1-11	188
„ viii. 39	177
„ xii. 1-8	194
„ xiii. 29	168, 186
„ xx. 19-26	206
Acts xi. 24	165
„ xi. 27-30	197
„ xx. 7	206
„ xx. 35	169
1 Corinthians i. 2	197

		PAGE		PAGE
1 Corinthians i. 26	.	210	Ephesians iv. 28 . .	167
„ iv. 7	.	200	„ v. 5-7 . .	226
„ v. 10, 11	.	226		
„ vi. 9, 10	.	226	1 Timothy iv. 8 . .	218
„ ix. 14	.	196	„ vi. 17 . .	204
„ xi. 34	.	196	„ vi. 18, 19 192, 210, 222	
„ xv. 58	.	199		
„ xvi. 1, 2	.	195	Hebrews vii. 4 . .	179
2 Corinthians viii. 1-3	.	239	James iv. 13-15 . .	204
„ viii. 8	.	163	2 Peter ii. 15, 16 . .	225
„ ix. 7, 9, 10		163		
			1 John ii. 15 . .	226
Galatians ii. 10	. .	168		
„ iii.	.	177, 178	Revelations i. 10 . .	206
„ vi. 7	. .	176	„ v. 12 . .	193

www.ingramcontent.com/pod-product-compliance
Lightning Source LLC
Chambersburg PA
CBHW020755230426
43666CB00007B/707